MongoDB
Data Modeling and Schema Design

Daniel Coupal

Pascal Desmarets

Steve Hoberman

Align > Refine > Design Series

Technics Publications

Published by:

115 Linda Vista, Sedona, AZ 86336 USA
https://www.TechnicsPub.com

Edited by Sadie Hoberman
Cover design by Lorena Molinari

First Printing 2023
Copyright © 2023 by Technics Publications

ISBN, print ed.	9781634621984
ISBN, Kindle ed.	9781634621991
ISBN, ePub ed.	9781634622127
ISBN, PDF ed.	9781634622134

Library of Congress Control Number: 2023934017

Contents

List of Figures

List of Tables

About the Book

My daughter can make a mean brownie. She starts with a store-bought brownie mix and adds chocolate chips, apple cider vinegar, and other "secret" ingredients to make her own unique delicious brownie.

Building a robust database design meeting users' needs requires a similar approach. The store-bought brownie mix represents a proven recipe for success. Likewise, there are data modeling practices that have proven successful over many decades. The chocolate chips and other secret ingredients represent the special additions that lead to an exceptional product. MongoDB has a number of special design considerations, much like the chocolate chips. Combining proven data modeling practices with MongoDB design-specific practices creates a series of data models representing powerful communication tools, greatly improving the opportunities for an exceptional design and application.

In fact, each book in the Align > Refine > Design series covers conceptual, logical, and physical data modeling for a specific database product, combining the best of data modeling practices with solution-specific design considerations. It is a winning combination.

My daughter's first few brownies were not a success, although as the proud (and hungry) dad, I ate them anyway—and they were still pretty tasty. It took practice to get the brownie to come out amazing. We need practice on the modeling side as well. Therefore, each book in the series follows the same animal shelter case study, allowing you to see the modeling techniques applied to reinforce your learning.

If you want to learn how to build multiple database solutions, read all the books in the series. Once you read one, you can pick up the techniques for another database solution even quicker.

Some say my first word was "data". I have been a data modeler for over 30 years and have taught variations of my **Data Modeling Master Class** since 1992—currently up to the 10th Edition! I have written nine books on data modeling, including *The Rosedata Stone* and *Data Modeling Made Simple*. I review data models using my Data Model Scorecard® technique. I am the founder of the Design Challenges group, creator of the Data Modeling Institute's Data Modeling Certification exam, Conference Chair of the Data Modeling Zone conferences, director of Technics Publications, lecturer at Columbia University, and recipient of the Data Administration Management Association (DAMA) International Professional Achievement Award.

Thinking of my daughter's brownie analogy, I have perfected the store-bought brownie recipe. That is, I know how to model. However, I am not an expert in every database solution.

That is why each book in this series combines my proven data modeling practices with database solution experts. So, for this book, Daniel Coupal, Pascal Desmarets, and I are making the brownie together. I work on the store-bought brownie piece, and Daniel and Pascal work on adding the chocolate chips and other delicious ingredients. Daniel and Pascal are MongoDB thought leaders.

Daniel Coupal is a Staff Engineer at MongoDB. He built the Data Modeling class for MongoDB University. He also defined a methodology to develop for MongoDB and created a series of Schema Design Patterns to optimize Data Modeling for MongoDB and other NoSQL databases.

Pascal Desmarets is the founder and CEO of Hackolade (https://hackolade.com), a data modeling tool for NoSQL databases, storage formats, REST APIs, and JSON in RDBMS. Hackolade pioneered Polyglot Data Modeling, which is data modeling for polyglot data persistence and data exchanges. With Hackolade's Metadata-as-Code strategy, data models are co-located with application code in Git repositories as they evolve and are published to business-facing data catalogs to ensure a shared understanding of the meaning and context of your data. We used Hackolade Studio software to create most of the entity-relationship diagrams in this book.

We hope our tag team approach shows you how to model any MongoDB solution. Particularly for those with experience in data modeling of relational databases, the book provides a bridge from the traditional methods to the very different way we model to leverage the benefits of NoSQL in general and MongoDB in particular.

MongoDB, the company, the products

MongoDB develops and provides a very popular open-source NoSQL document-oriented database. MongoDB uses JSON-like documents with optional schemas, which allows for the storage and retrieval of data in a flexible and scalable manner. MongoDB is designed to handle large amounts of data and provides high performance and scalability. The database supports a wide variety of data types, including text, numbers, decimals, and binary data, and it allows for storing unstructured and semi-structured data.

In addition to the MongoDB database, MongoDB Inc. also offers several other products and services:

- **MongoDB Atlas**: A fully managed cloud-based version of MongoDB so developers can easily deploy, operate, and scale MongoDB on various cloud providers, such as AWS, Azure, and GCP. The MongoDB Atlas developer data platform includes a Data Lake, data archiving, triggers, and many more functionalities.

- **MongoDB Charts**: A data visualization tool so users can create charts, dashboards, and reports based on data stored in MongoDB.

- **MongoDB Compass**: A graphical user interface (GUI) for MongoDB that allows users to easily visualize, query, and manage MongoDB data.

- **MongoDB Realm**: A platform for building serverless and offline-capable mobile and web applications that integrates with MongoDB and other services.

- **MongoDB Connectors**: These are connectors that allow MongoDB to integrate with other systems and technologies like BI tools, ETL, data integration, and graph processing.

MongoDB is widely adopted by companies of all sizes, in various industries, and is supported by a large and active community of developers. MongoDB Inc. provides various support options and services to help customers in their use of MongoDB.

The document model of MongoDB

In MongoDB, the document model refers to the way data is organized and stored within the database. Data is stored in the form of documents formatted using the BSON (Binary JSON) specification (https://bsonspec.org/). Each document is made of key-value pairs, similar to a JSON object. A document is the basic unit of data (like a row in a relational database) and can include nesting to represent complex data structures.

A collection in MongoDB is a group of documents, and is similar to a table in relational technology. A collection can store an extremely large set of documents, and it is possible to store documents with a different set of fields inside the same collection. Developers embrace the document model in MongoDB because it is flexible and can dynamically evolve. As we will see in the book, this power comes with great responsibility, as it can easily become messy if not managed carefully.

Two key features in a document-oriented database not found in tabular rows of Relational Database Management Systems (RDBMS) are hierarchical structures and polymorphism.[1] Let's review each.

Hierarchical structure in documents

Documents can represent data in a nested or hierarchical structure. This is in contrast with RDBMS tables, which are

---

[1] Relational databases have increasingly added support for JSON. But the capabilities are not the same as a pure document database, because in RDBMS, JSON payload is stored as a blob (or a varchar(4000)). As a result it lacks the indexing and query capabilities of MongoDB. PostgreSQL with its JSONB datatype is attempting to bridge that gap.

a two-dimensional tabular grid of columns and rows, and require the use of relationships and joins to represent hierarchical data. In JSON documents, data can be nested within other data, creating a tree-like structure.

Aside from the traditional "scalar" data types (string, numeric, Boolean, null), it is possible to use what is known as "complex" data types: objects and arrays. In JSON, an object is a collection of key-value pairs enclosed in curly braces {}. See Figure 1.

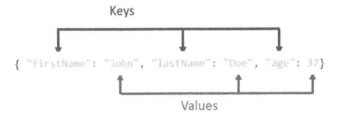

Figure 1: JSON object.

The keys are always strings, and the values can be any valid JSON data type, including another object, an array, a string, a number, a Boolean, or null.

```
{
   "name": "John Smith",
   "age": 35,
   "address": {
     "street": "123 Main St",
     "city": "Anytown",
     "state": "CA",
     "zip": "12345"
   }
}
```

Note that there are more data types in MongoDB, given that it uses the BSON specification, including ObjectID, ISODate, integer, floating point, decimal, regex, UUID, etc.

An array is an ordered list of values enclosed in square brackets []. The values can be any valid JSON data type, including another array, an object, a string, a number, a Boolean, or null. Each value in the array is separated by a comma.

```
["apple",  "banana",  "orange",  "grape"]
```

You can combine objects and arrays at will, as shown in Figure 2.

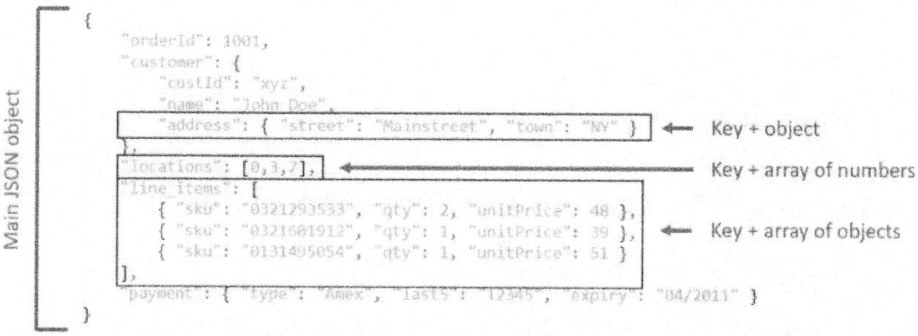

Figure 2: Combining objects at will.

For example, you may use an array of objects to embed another table into a collection. The array models the one-to-many or many-to-many relationship between the two tables.

Generally, in a JSON key-value pair, the key is a static name. It is also possible to have variable names for the key:

```
{
    "followers": {
        "abc123": {
            "name": "John Doe",
            "sports": ["tennis"]
        },
        "xyz987": {
            "name": "Joe Blow",
            "sports": ["cycling", "football"]
        }
    }
}
```

This advanced feature, sometimes called "pattern properties" or "unpredictable keys", is a special case of the attribute pattern detailed below. Hackolade Studio correctly maintains and also detects these structures during the schema inference of a reverse-engineering process, but traditional SQL and BI tools are challenged by these unusual structures.

Grouping data in JSON with hierarchical subobjects and arrays can provide several benefits:

- **Improved data organization**: nesting related data with subobjects and arrays makes it easier to understand, navigate, query, and manipulate data.

- **Flexibility**: a more flexible data model can evolve and adapt to changing requirements more easily.

- **Improved performance**: embedding subdocuments within a parent document can improve performance by reducing the number of joins required to retrieve the data.

- **Better data representation**: for example, a customer object can contain a nested address object. In this way, it is clear that the address is related to the customer and it is also more readable and intuitive.

- **Data integrity**: by keeping related data together, for example, each order can contain an array of cart items. This way it is clear that the orders and items are related, and it is also easy to update all related data when it is required, and perform cascading deletes.

- **Developer convenience**: by aggregating structures to match objects to be manipulated in object-oriented programming, developers are more efficient by avoiding what's known as "object impedance mismatch", a common issue when working with relational databases.

To fully visualize the above benefits and why users embrace the document model of MongoDB as an intuitive alternative to the traditional relational database structures, let's use the simple example of an order.

With a relational database respecting the rules of normalization, we split the different components of an order into different tables at storage time. And when retrieving the data, joins are used to reassemble the different pieces for processing, display, or reporting. This is counter-intuitive for the common human (i.e., someone not trained in Third Normal Form) and expensive in terms of performance, particularly at scale. See Figure 3.

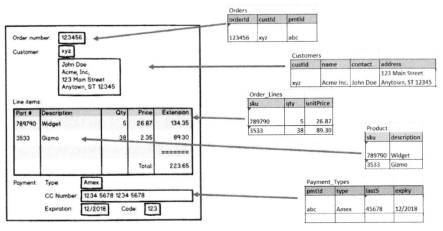

Figure 3: Normalization example.

With a JSON document, however, all the pieces of information that belong together are stored and retrieved together in a single document, an example appearing in Figure 4.

Nesting can provide the benefits described above, but it can also sometimes make data more complex and harder to work with if it's not properly organized and structured. And since there are no rules of normalization to serve as guardrails, data modeling is even more important than with relational databases.

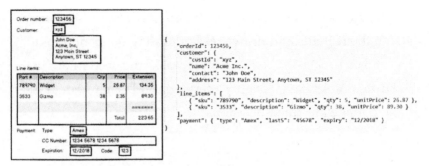

Figure 4: JSON example.

Nesting subobjects and arrays to denormalize data to represent relationships can also increase the storage requirements, but with the minimal cost of storage these days, this drawback is often considered marginal.

Just like XSD defines elements and structures that can appear in XML documents, JSON Schema (https://json-schema.org/) defines how a JSON document should be structured, making it easy to ensure that it is formatted correctly. When used in the context of the MongoDB validator (https://www.mongodb.com/docs/manual/core/schema-validation/), you can enforce the specified schema on insert and update operations in MongoDB for higher consistency and data quality. Hackolade Studio uses JSON Schema as an internal notation mechanism, so it dynamically generates JSON Schema for structures created with the tool, as well as the MongoDB Validator script, without the need for the user to be familiar with the JSON Schema syntax.

To decide whether to use or avoid, developers should weigh the benefits and drawbacks of nesting data and make an informed decision. Later in this book, the section about the different schema design patterns provides many details to help make informed decisions.

Polymorphism

Polymorphism in JSON refers to the ability of a JSON object to take on multiple forms.

Fields with multiple data types

The simplest case of polymorphism in JSON is when a field can have different data types, for example:

```
{
  "raceResults": [
        {
          "Position": 1,
          "Driver": "Lewis Hamilton"
        },
        {
          "Position": 2,
          "Driver": "Max Verstappen"
        },
        {
          "Position": "DNF",
          "Driver": "Charles Leclerc"
        }
    ]
}
```

The "Position" field can have different data types (numeric or string) depending on the race result.

Multiple document types in the same collection

A more complex case of polymorphism is when different documents in the same collection have different shapes, similar to table inheritance in relational databases. Specifically, it refers to the ability of a JSON object to have different properties or fields, depending on the type of data it represents.

For example, consider a collection for bank accounts. Several types of bank accounts are possible: checking, savings, and loan. There is a structure common to all types, and a structure specific to each type. For example, a document for a checking account might look like this:

```
{
  "accountNumber": "123456789",
  "balance": 1000,
  "accountType": "checking",
  "accountDetails": {
    "minimumBalance": 100,
    "overdraftLimit": 500
  }
}
```

Another document for a savings account might look like this:

```
{
```

```
  "accountNumber": "987654321",
  "balance": 5000,
  "accountType": "savings",
  "accountDetails": {
    "interestRate": 0.05,
    "interestEarned": 115.26
  }
}
```

And for a loan account, a document might look like this:

```
{
  "accountNumber": "567890123",
  "balance": -5916.06,
  "accountType": "loan",
  "accountDetails": {
    "loanAmount": 10000,
    "term": 36,
    "interestRate": 1.5,
    "monthlyPmt": 291.71
  }
}
```

This flexible and dynamic structure is very convenient and eliminates the need for separate tables or wide tables that would quickly become unmanageable at scale.

However, this flexibility can also create challenges when querying or manipulating the data, as it requires applications to account for variations in data types and structure. Without going into details at this stage, Figure 5 shows a single schema for these documents.

Figure 5: Single schema.

For those familiar with traditional data modeling, the above would be represented with subtypes and could result in table inheritance, as shown in Figure 6.

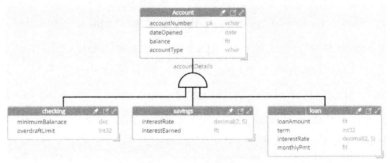

Figure 6: Subtyping.

Schema evolution and versioning

Another common case of polymorphism is when documents have different shapes within the same collection, due to the progressive evolution of the document schema over time. This could be done implicitly, or with an explicit version number as part of the root-level fields of the document.

Developers love the fact that schema evolution is easy with MongoDB. You can add or remove fields, change data types, modify indexing options, etc., to accommodate new or changing requirements without the headaches that such changes would imply with relational databases.

The schema versioning pattern is described in detail later in this book. For now, it is enough to know that this pattern leverages the polymorphic capabilities of the document model.

We should manage schema evolution and versioning carefully to avoid technical debt and to consider that data may be read by different applications and SQL or BI tools that may be unable to handle this polymorphism. Schema migration is a best practice in successful projects and organizations leveraging NoSQL, and, therefore, should be part of the schema evolution strategy to mitigate the drawbacks.

Data modeling and schema design

As you can imagine, data modeling and schema design for MongoDB is very different than for relational databases. That's because MongoDB stores JSON-like documents as denormalized documents with nested objects and arrays instead of normalized flat tables. And also because MongoDB does not impose a fixed schema to be enforced by the database engine like a traditional RDBMS.

The flexibility of the document approach is a fantastic opportunity that many developers love. But this flexibility comes with some risks. As MongoDB does not enforce constraints, it is up to the developers to ensure that data remains consistent and conforms to application requirements. Failing to do so could lead to data corruption, inaccurate query results, and application errors. Data modeling helps mitigate these risks with a proactive approach to ensure that data is consistent and of high quality. It also contributes to higher productivity and lower Total Cost of Ownership (TCO). And with a modern approach to data modeling and next-gen tooling born in the 21st century, it fits right into your Agile development process.

Data modeling is a crucial step in the development process, as it allows developers to work closely with subject matter experts to define the structure of the data before any coding begins. Just as a recipe is used to guide the baking of brownies, a data model serves as a blueprint for the structure and organization of data. By involving subject matter experts in the modeling process, developers can ensure that the data model accurately reflects the needs and requirements of the project. With such collaboration, developers are more likely to avoid potential mistakes and inconsistencies that could arise from working with poorly defined data. By following a recipe before starting to bake, developers can be more efficient and successful in creating a product that meets the needs of the end-user.

Audience

We wrote this book for two audiences:

- Data architects and modelers who need to expand their modeling skills to include MongoDB. That is, those of us who know how to make a store-bought brownie but are looking for those secret additions like chocolate chips.

- Database administrators and developers who know MongoDB but need to expand their modeling skills. That is, those of us who know the value of chocolate chips and other ingredients, but need to learn how to combine these ingredients with those store-bought brownie mixes.

This book contains a foundational introduction followed by three approach-driven chapters. Think of the introduction as making that store-built brownie and the subsequent chapters as adding chocolate chips and other yummy ingredients. More on these four sections:

- **Introduction: About Data Models**. This overview covers the three modeling characteristics of precise, minimal, and visual; the three model components of entities, relationships, and attributes; the three model levels of conceptual (align), logical (refine), and physical (design); and the three modeling perspectives of relational, dimensional, and query. By the end of this introduction, you will know data modeling concepts and how to approach any data modeling assignment. This introduction will be useful to database administrators and developers who need a foundation in data modeling, as well as data architects and data modelers who need a modeling refresher.

- **Chapter 1: Align**. This chapter will explain the data modeling align phase. We explain the purpose of aligning our business vocabulary, introduce our animal shelter case study, and then walk through the align approach. This chapter will be useful for both audiences, architects/modelers and database administrators/developers.

- **Chapter 2: Refine**. This chapter will explain the data modeling refine phase. We explain the purpose of refine, refine the model for our animal shelter case study, and then walk through the refine approach. This chapter will be useful for both audiences, architects/modelers and database administrators/developers.

- **Chapter 3: Design**. This chapter will explain the data modeling design phase. We explain the purpose of design, design the model for our animal shelter case study, and then walk through the design approach. This chapter will be useful for both audiences, architects/modelers and database administrators/developers.

We end each chapter with three tips and three takeaways. We aim to write as concisely yet comprehensively as possible to make the most of your time.

Most data models throughout the book were created using Hackolade Studio (https://hackolade.com) and are accessible for reference at https://github.com/hackolade/books along with additional sample data models to play with.

Let's begin!

Daniel, Pascal, and Steve

About Data Models

This chapter is all about making that store-built brownie. We present the data modeling principles and concepts within a single chapter. In addition to explaining the data model, this chapter covers the three modeling characteristics of precise, minimal, and visual; the three model components of entities, relationships, and attributes; the three model levels of conceptual (align), logical (refine), and physical (design); and the three modeling perspectives of relational, dimensional, and query. By the end of this chapter, you will know how to approach any data modeling assignment.

Data model explanation

A model is a precise representation of a landscape. Precise means there is only one way to read a model—it is not ambiguous nor up to interpretation. You and I read the same model the exact same way, making the model an extremely valuable communication tool.

We need to 'speak' a language before we can discuss content. That is, once we know how to read the symbols on a model (syntax), we can discuss what the symbols represent (semantics).

Once we understand the syntax, we can discuss the semantics.

For example, a map like the one in Figure 7 helps a visitor navigate a city. Once we know what the symbols mean on a map, such as lines representing streets, we can read the map and use it as a valuable navigation tool for understanding a geographical landscape.

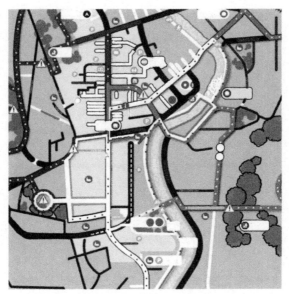

Figure 7: Map of a geographic landscape.

A blueprint like the one in Figure 8 helps an architect communicate building plans. The blueprint, too, contains only representations, such as rectangles for rooms and lines for pipes. Once we know what the rectangles and lines mean on a blueprint, we know what the structure will look like and can understand the architectural landscape.

The data model like the one in Figure 9 helps business and technologists discuss requirements and terminology. The data model, too, contains only representations, such as rectangles for terms and lines for business rules. Once we know what the rectangles and lines mean on a data model, we can debate and eventually agree on the business requirements and terminology captured in the informational landscape.

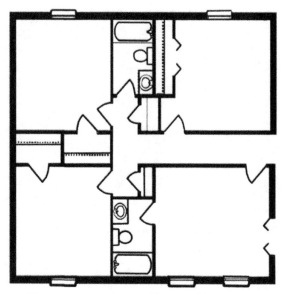

Figure 8: Map of an architectural landscape.

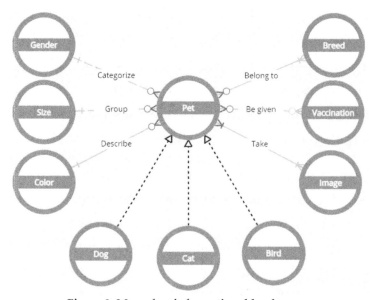

Figure 9: Map of an informational landscape.

A data model is a precise representation of an information landscape. We build data models to confirm and document our understanding of other perspectives.

In addition to precision, two other important characteristics of the model are minimal and visual. Let's discuss all three characteristics.

Three model characteristics

Models are valuable because they are precise—there is only one way to interpret the symbols on the model. We must transform the ambiguity in our verbal and sometimes written communication into a precise language. Precision does not mean complex—we need to keep our language simple and show the minimal amount needed for successful communication. In addition, following the maxim "a picture is worth a thousand words," we need visuals to communicate this precise and simple language for the initiative.

Precise, minimal, and visual are three essential characteristics of the model.

Precise

Bob: How's your course going?

Mary: Going well. But my students are complaining about too much homework. They tell me they have many other classes.

Bob: The attendees in my advanced session say the same thing.

Mary: I wouldn't expect that from graduates. Anyway, how many other offerings are you teaching this semester?

Bob: I'm teaching five offerings this term and one is an evening not-for-credit class.

We can let this conversation continue for a few pages, but do you see the ambiguity caused by this simple dialog?

- What is the difference between **Course, Class, Offering,** and **Session**?
- Are **Semester** and **Term** the same?
- Are **Student** and **Attendee** the same?

Precision means "exactly or sharply defined or stated." Precision means there is only one interpretation for a term, including the term's name, definition, and connections to other terms. Most issues organizations face related to growth, credibility, and saving lives, stem from a lack of precision.

On a recent project, Steve needed to explain data modeling to a group of senior human resource executives. These very high-level managers lead departments responsible for implementing a very expensive global employee expense system. Steve felt the last thing these busy human resource executives needed was a lecture on data modeling. So instead, he asked each of these managers sitting around this large boardroom table to write down their definition of an employee. After a few minutes, most of the writing stopped and he asked them to share their definitions of an employee.

As expected, no two definitions were the same. For example, one manager included contingency workers in his definition, while another included summer interns. Instead of spending the remaining meeting time attempting to come to a consensus on the meaning of an employee, we discussed the reasons we create data models, including the value of precision. Steve explained that after we complete the difficult journey of achieving the agreed-upon employee definition and document it in the form of a data model, no one will ever have to go through the same painful process again. Instead, they can use and build upon the existing model, adding even more value for the organization.

Making terms precise is hard work. We need to transform the ambiguity in our verbal and sometimes written communication into a form where five people can read about the term and each gets a single clear picture of the term, not five different interpretations. For example, a group of business users initially define **Product** as:

Something we produce intending to sell for profit.

Is this definition precise? If you and I read this definition, are we each clear on what *something* means? Is *something* tangible like a hammer or instead some type of service? If it is a hammer and we donate this hammer to a not-for-profit organization, is it still a hammer? After all, we didn't make a *profit* on it. The word *intending* may cover us, but still, shouldn't this word be explained in more detail? And who is *we*? Is it our entire organization or maybe just a subset? What does *profit* really mean anyway? Can two people read the word *profit* and see it very differently?

You see the problem. We need to think like a detective to find gaps and ambiguous statements in the text to make terms precise. After some debate, we update our **Product** definition to:

A product, also known as a finished product, is something that is in a state to be sold to a consumer. It has completed the manufacturing process, contains a wrapper, and is labeled for resale. A product is different than a raw material and a semi-finished good. A raw material such as sugar or milk, and a semi-finished good such as melted chocolate is never sold to a consumer. If in the future, sugar or milk is sold directly to consumers, than sugar and milk become products.

Examples:
Widgets Dark Chocolate 42 oz
Lemonizer 10 oz
Blueberry pickle juice 24 oz

Ask at least five people to see if they are all clear on this particular initiative's definition of a product. The best way to test precision is to try to break the definition. Think of lots of examples and see if everyone makes the same decision as to whether the examples are products or not.

In 1967, G.H. Mealy wrote a white paper where he made this statement:

> We do not, it seems, have a very clear and commonly agreed upon set of notions about data—either what they are, how they should be fed and cared for, or their relation to the design of programming languages and operating systems.[2]

Although Mr. Mealy made this claim over 50 years ago, if we replace *programming languages and operating systems* with the word *databases*, we can make a similar claim today.

Aiming for precision can help us better understand our business terms and business requirements.

Minimal

The world around us is full of obstacles that can overwhelm our senses, making it very challenging to focus only on the relevant information needed to make intelligent decisions. Therefore, the model contains a minimal set of symbols and text, simplifying a subset of the real world by only including representations of what we need to understand. Much is filtered out on a model, creating an incomplete but extremely useful reflection of

---

[2] G. H. Mealy, "Another Look at Data," AFIPS, pp. 525-534, 1967 Proceedings of the Fall Joint Computer Conference, 1967. http://tw.rpi.edu/media/2013/11/11/134fa/GHMealy-1967-FJCC-p525.pdf.

reality. For example, we might need to communicate descriptive information about **Customer**, such as their name, birth date, and email address. But we will not include information on the process of adding or deleting a customer.

Visuals

Visuals mean that we need a picture instead of lots of text. Our brains process images 60,000 times faster than text, and 90 percent of the information transmitted to the brain is visual.[3]

We might read an entire document but not reach that moment of clarity until we see a figure or picture summarizing everything. Imagine reading directions to navigate from one city to another versus the ease of reading a map that shows visually how the roads connect.

Three model components

The three components of a data model are entities, relationships, and attributes (including keys).

---

[3] https://www.t-sciences.com/news/humans-process-visual-data-better.

Entities

An entity is a collection of information about something important to the business. It is a noun considered basic and critical to your audience for a particular initiative. Basic means this entity is mentioned frequently in conversations while discussing the initiative. Critical means the initiative would be very different or non-existent without this entity.

The majority of entities are easy to identify and include nouns that are common across industries, such as **Customer**, **Employee**, and **Product**. Entities can have different names and meanings within departments, organizations, or industries based on audience and initiative (scope). An airline may call a **Customer** a *Passenger*, a hospital may call a **Customer** a *Patient*, an insurance company may call a **Customer** a *Policyholder*, yet they are all recipients of goods or services.

Each entity fits into one of six categories: who, what, when, where, why, or how. That is, each entity is either a who, what, when, where, why, or how. Table 1 contains a definition of each of these categories, along with examples.

Category	Definition	Examples
Who	Person or organization of interest to the initiative.	Employee, Patient, Player, Suspect, Customer, Vendor, Student, Passenger, Competitor, Author
What	Product or service of interest to the initiative. What the organization makes or provides that keeps it in business.	Product, Service, Raw Material, Finished Good, Course, Song, Photograph, Tax Preparation, Policy, Breed
When	Calendar or time interval of interest to the initiative.	Schedule, Semester, Fiscal Period, Duration
Where	Location of interest to the initiative. Location can refer to actual places as well as electronic places.	Employee Home Address, Distribution Point, Customer Website
Why	Event or transaction of interest to the initiative.	Order, Return, Complaint, Withdrawal, Payment, Trade, Claim
How	Documentation of the event of interest to the initiative. Records events such as a Purchase Order (a "How") recording an Order event (a "Why"). A document provides evidence that an event took place.	Invoice, Contract, Agreement, Purchase Order, Speeding Ticket, Packing Slip, Trade Confirmation

Table 1: Entity categories plus examples.

Entities are traditionally shown as rectangles on a data model, such as these two for our animal shelter:

```
Pet                    Breed
```

Figure 10: Traditional entities.

Entity instances are the occurrences, examples, or representatives of that entity. The entity **Pet** may have multiple instances, such as Spot, Daisy, and Misty. The entity **Breed** may have multiple instances, such as German Shephard, Greyhound, and Beagle.

Entities and entity instances take on more precise names when discussing specific technologies. For example, entities are tables and instances are rows in a RDBMS like Oracle. Entities are collections and instances are documents in MongoDB.

Relationships

A relationship represents a business connection between two entities, and appears on the model traditionally as a line connecting two rectangles. For example, here is a relationship between **Pet** and **Breed**:

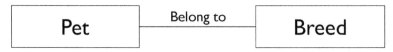

Figure 11: Relationship and label.

The phrase **Belong to** is called a *label*. A label adds meaning to the relationship. Instead of just saying that a

Pet may relate to a **Breed**, we can say that a **Pet** may belong to a **Breed**. **Belong to** is more meaningful than **Relate**.

So far, we know that a relationship represents a business connection between two entities. It would be nice to know more about the relationship, such as whether a **Pet** may belong to more than one **Breed** or whether a **Breed** can categorize more than one **Pet**. Enter cardinality.

Cardinality means the additional symbols on the relationship line that communicate how many instances from one entity participate in the relationship with instances of the other entity.

There are several modeling notations, and each notation has its own set of symbols. Throughout this book, we use a notation called *Information Engineering (IE)*. The IE notation has been a very popular notation since the early 1980s. If you use a notation other than IE within your organization, you must translate the following symbols into the corresponding symbols in your modeling notation.

We can choose any combination of zero, one, or many for cardinality. *Many* (some people use "more") means one or more. Yes, many includes one. Specifying one or many allows us to capture *how many* of a particular entity instance participate in a given relationship. Specifying zero or one allows us to capture whether an entity instance is or is not required in a relationship.

Recall this relationship between **Pet** and **Breed**:

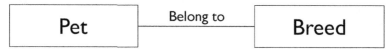

Figure 12: Relationship and label.

Let's now add cardinality.

We first ask the *Participation* questions to learn more. Participation questions tell us whether the relationship is 'one' or 'many'. So, for example:

- Can a **Pet** belong to more than one **Breed**?
- Can a **Breed** categorize more than one **Pet**?

A simple spreadsheet can keep track of these questions and their answers:

Question	Yes	No
Can a Pet belong to more than one Breed?		
Can a Breed categorize more than one Pet?		

We asked the animal shelter experts and received these answers:

Question	Yes	No
Can a Pet belong to more than one Breed?	✓	
Can a Breed categorize more than one Pet?	✓	

We learn that a **Pet** may belong to more than one **Breed**. For example, Daisy is part Beagle and part Terrier. We also learned that a **Breed** may categorize more than one **Pet**. Both Sparky and Spot are Greyhounds.

'Many' (meaning one or more) on a data model in the IE notation is a symbol that looks like a crow's foot (and is called a *crow's foot* by data folks). See Figure 13.

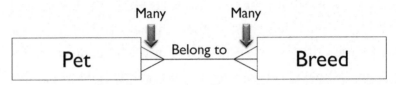

Figure 13: Displaying the answers to the Participation questions.

Now we know more about the relationship:

- Each **Pet** may belong to many **Breeds**.
- Each **Breed** may categorize many **Pets**.

We also always use the word 'each' when reading a relationship and start with the entity that makes the most sense to the reader, usually the one with the clearest relationship label.

This relationship is not yet precise, though. So, in addition to asking these two Participation questions, we also need to ask the *Existence* questions. Existence tells us for each relationship whether one entity can exist without the other term. For example:

- Can a **Pet** exist without a **Breed**?
- Can a **Breed** exist without a **Pet**?

We asked the animal shelter experts and received these answers:

Question	Yes	No
Can a Pet exist without a Breed?		✓
Can a Breed exist without a Pet?	✓	

So we learn that a **Pet** cannot exist without a **Breed**, and that a **Breed** can exist without a **Pet**. This means, for example, that we may not have any Chihuahuas in our animal shelter. Yet we need to capture a **Breed** (and in this case, one or more **Breeds**), for every **Pet**. As soon as we know about Daisy, we need to identify at least one of her breeds, such as Beagle or Terrier.

Figure 14 displays the answers to these two questions.

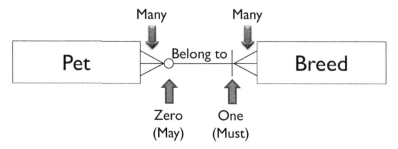

Figure 14: Displaying the answers to the Existence questions.

After adding existence, we have a precise relationship:

- Each **Pet** must belong to many **Breeds**.
- Each **Breed** may categorize many **Pets**.

The Existence questions are also known as the May/Must questions. The Existence questions tell us when reading the relationship, whether we say "may" or "must." A zero means "may", indicating optionality—the entity can exist without the other entity. A **Breed** *may* exist without a **Pet**, for example. A one means "must", indicating required—the entity cannot exist without the other entity. A **Pet** *must* belong to at least one **Breed**, for example.

There are two more questions that need to be asked if we are working on the more detailed logical data model (which will be discussed shortly). These are the *Identification* questions.

Identification tells us for each relationship whether one entity can be identified without the other term. For example:

- Can a **Pet** be identified without a **Breed**?
- Can a **Breed** be identified without a **Pet**?

We asked the animal shelter experts and received these answers:

Question	Yes	No
Can a Pet be identified without a Breed?	✓	
Can a Breed be identified without a Pet?	✓	

So we learn that a **Pet** can be identified without knowing a **Breed**. We can identify the pet Sparky without knowing that Sparky is a German Shepherd. In addition, we can identify a **Breed** without knowing the **Pet**. This means, for example, that we can identify the Chihuahua breed without including any information from **Pet**.

A dotted line captures a non-identifying relationship. That is, when the answer to both questions is "yes". A solid line captures an identifying relationship. That is, when one of the answers is "no".

Non-identifying

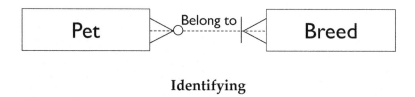

Identifying

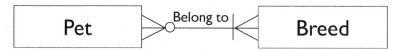

Figure 15: A non-identifying (top) and identifying (bottom) relationship.

So to summarize, the Participation questions reveal whether each entity has a one or many relationship to the other entity. The Existence questions reveal whether each entity has an optional ("may") or mandatory ("must") relationship to the other entity. The Identification questions reveal whether each entity requires the other entity to bring back a unique entity instance.

Use instances to make things clear in the beginning and eventually help you explain your models to colleagues. See Figure 16 for an example.

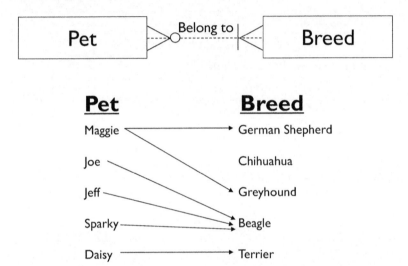

Figure 16: Use sample data to validate a relationship.

You can see from this dataset that a **Pet** can belong to more than one **Breed**, such as Maggie being a German Shepherd/Greyhound mix. You can also see that every **Pet** must belong to at least one **Breed**. We could also have a **Breed** that is not categorizing any **Pets**, such as Chihuahua. In addition, a **Breed** can categorize multiple **Pets**, such as Joe, Jeff, and Sparky are all Beagles.

Answering all six questions leads to a precise relationship. Precise means we all read the model the same exact way.

Let's say that we have slightly different answers to our six questions:

Question	Yes	No
Can a Pet belong to more than one Breed?		✓
Can a Breed categorize more than one Pet?	✓	
Can a Pet exist without a Breed?		✓
Can a Breed exist without a Pet?	✓	
Can a Pet be identified without a Breed?	✓	
Can a Breed be identified without a Pet?	✓	

These six answers lead to this model:

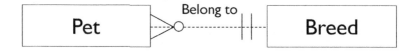

- Each **Pet** must belong to one **Breed**.
- Each **Breed** may categorize many **Pets**.

Figure 17: Different answers to the six questions lead to different cardinality.

On this model, we are only including pure-breed pets, as a **Pet** must be assigned one **Breed**. No mutts in our shelter!

Be very clear on labels. Labels are the verbs that connect our entities (nouns). To read any complete sentence, we need both nouns and verbs. Make sure the labels on the relationship lines are as descriptive as possible. Here are some examples of good labels:

- Contain
- Provide
- Own
- Initiate
- Characterize

Avoid the following words as labels, as they provide no additional information to the reader. You can use these words in combination with other words to make a meaningful label; just avoid using these words by themselves:

- Have
- Associate
- Participate
- Relate
- Are

For example, replace the relationship sentence:

"Each **Pet** must *relate to* one **Breed**."

With:

"Each **Pet** must *belong to* one **Breed**."

Relationships take on more precise names when discussing specific technologies. For example, relationships are constraints in a RDBMS such as Oracle. Relationships in MongoDB can be represented with references, but they are not enforceable constraints. It is often preferred to implement relationships through embedding. The pros and cons of both approaches are discussed at length later in the book.

In addition to relationship lines, we can also have a subtyping relationship. The subtyping relationship groups common entities together. For example, the **Dog** and **Cat** entities might be grouped using subtyping under the more generic **Pet** term. In this example, **Pet** would be called the grouping entity or supertype, and **Dog** and **Cat** would be the terms that are grouped together, also known as the subtypes, as shown in Figure 18.

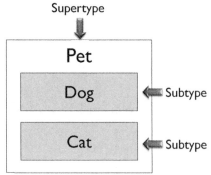

Figure 18: Subtyping is similar to the concept of inheritance.

We would read this model as:

- Each **Pet** may be either a **Dog** or a **Cat**.
- **Dog** is a **Pet**. **Cat** is a **Pet**.

The subtyping relationship means that all of the relationships (and attributes that we'll learn about shortly) that belong to the supertype from other terms also belong to each subtype. Therefore, the relationships to **Pet** also belong to **Dog** and **Cat**. So, for example, cats can be assigned breeds as well, so the relationship to **Breed** can exist at the **Pet** level instead of the **Dog** level, encompassing both cats and dogs. See Figure 19 for an example.

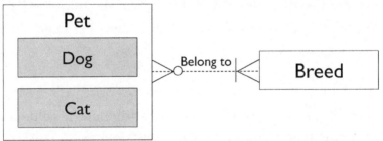

Figure 19: The relationship to Pet is inherited to Dog and Cat.

So the relationship:

- Each **Pet** must belong to many **Breeds**.
- Each **Breed** may categorize many **Pets**.

Also applies to **Dog** and **Cat**:

- Each **Dog** must belong to many **Breeds**.
- Each **Breed** may categorize many **Dogs**.
- Each **Cat** must belong to many **Breeds**.
- Each **Breed** may categorize many **Cats**.

Not only does subtyping reduce redundancy, but it also makes it easier to communicate similarities across what would appear to be distinct and separate terms.

Attributes and keys

An entity contains attributes. An *attribute* is an individual piece of information whose values identify, describe, or measure instances of an entity. The entity **Pet** might contain the attributes **Pet Number** that identifies the **Pet**, **Pet Name** that describes the **Pet**, and **Pet Age** that measures the **Pet.**

Attributes take on more precise names when discussing specific technologies. For example, attributes are columns in a RDBMS such as Oracle. Attributes are fields in MongoDB.

A candidate key is one or more attributes that uniquely identify an entity instance. We assign a **ISBN** (International Standard Book Number) to every title. The **ISBN** uniquely identifies each title and is, therefore, the title's candidate key. **Tax ID** can be a candidate key for an organization in some countries, such as the United States. **Account Code** can be a candidate key for an account. A **VIN** (Vehicle Identification Number) identifies a vehicle.

A candidate key must be unique and mandatory. Unique means a candidate key value must not identify more than one entity instance (or one real-world thing). Mandatory means a candidate key cannot be empty (also known as *nullable*). Each entity instance must be identified by exactly one candidate key value.

The number of distinct values of a candidate key is always equal to the number of distinct entity instances. If the entity **Title** has **ISBN** as its candidate key, and if there are 500 title instances, there will also be 500 unique ISBNs.

Even though an entity may contain more than one candidate key, we can only select one candidate key to be the primary key for an entity. A primary key is the candidate key that has been chosen to be *the preferred* unique identifier for an entity. An alternate key is a candidate key that, although it has the properties of being unique and mandatory, was not chosen as the primary key though it may still be used to find specific entity instances.

The primary key appears above the line in the entity box, and the alternate key contains the 'AK' in parentheses. So in the following **Pet** entity, **Pet Number** is the primary key and **Pet Name** is the alternate key. Having an alternate key on **Pet Name** means we cannot have two pets with the same name. Whether this can happen or not is a good discussion point. However, the model in its current state would not allow duplicate **Pet Names**.

Figure 20: An alternate key on Pet Name means we cannot have two pets with the same name.

A candidate key can be either simple, compound, or composite. If it is simple, it can be either business or surrogate. Table 2 contains examples of each key type.

	SIMPLE	COMPOUND	COMPOSITE	OVERLOADED
BUSINESS	ISBN	PROMOTION TYPE CODE PROMOTION START DATE	(CUSTOMER FIRST NAME + CUSTOMER LAST NAME + BIRTHDAY)	STUDENT GRADE
SURROGATE	BOOK ID			

Table 2: Examples of each key type.

Sometimes a single attribute identifies an entity instance, such as **ISBN** for a title. When a single attribute makes up a key, we use the term *simple key*. A simple key can either be a business (also called natural) key or a surrogate key.

A business key is visible to the business (such as **Policy Number** for a **Policy**). A surrogate key is never visible to the business. A surrogate key is created by a technologist to help with a technology issue, such as space efficiency, speed, or integration. It is a unique identifier for a table, often a counter, usually fixed-size, and always system-generated without intelligence, so a surrogate key carries no business meaning.

Sometimes it takes more than one attribute to uniquely identify an entity instance. For example, both a **Promotion Type Code** and **Promotion Start Date** may be necessary to identify a promotion. When more than one attribute makes up a key, we use the term *compound key*. Therefore, **Promotion Type Code** and **Promotion Start Date** together are a compound candidate key for a promotion. When a key contains more than one piece of information, we use the term *composite key*. A simple key that includes the customer's first name, last name, and birthday, all in the same attribute, would be an example of a simple composite key. When a key contains different attributes, it is called an *overloaded* key. A **Student Grade** attribute might sometimes contain the actual grade, such as A, B, or C. At other times it might just contain a P for Pass and F for Fail. **Student Grade**, therefore, would be an overloaded attribute. **Student Grade** sometimes contains the student's grade, and other times indicates whether the student has passed the class.

Let's look at the model in Figure 21.

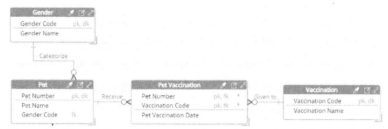

Figure 21: The entity on the many side contains a foreign key pointing back to the primary key from the entity on the one side.

Here are the rules captured on this model:

- Each **Gender** may categorize many **Pets**.
- Each **Pet** must be categorized by one **Gender**.
- Each **Pet** may Receive many **Vaccinations**.
- Each **Vaccination** may be given to many **Pets**.

The entity on the "one" side of the relationship is called the parent entity, and the entity on the "many" side of the relationship is called the child entity. For example, in the relationship between **Gender** and **Pet**, **Gender** is the parent and **Pet** is the child. When we create a relationship from a parent entity to a child entity, the parent's primary key is copied as a foreign key to the child. You can see the foreign key, **Gender Code**, in the **Pet** entity.

A foreign key is one or more attributes that link to another entity (or, in a case of a recursive relationship where two instances of the same entity may be related, that is, a relationship that starts and ends with the same entity, a link to the same entity). At the physical level, a foreign key allows a relational database management system to navigate from one table to another. For example, if we need to know the **Gender** of a particular **Pet**, we can use the **Gender Code** foreign key in **Pet** to navigate to the parent **Gender**.

Three model levels

Traditionally, data modeling produces a set of structures for a Relational Database Management System (RDBMS). First, we build the Conceptual Data Model (CDM) (more appropriately called the Business Terms Model or BTM for short) to capture the common business language for the initiative (e.g., "What's a Customer?"). Next, we create the Logical Data Model (LDM) using the BTM's common business language to precisely define the business requirements (e.g., "I need to see the customer's name and address on this report."). Finally, in the Physical Data Model (PDM), we design these business requirements specific for a particular technology such as Oracle, Teradata, or SQL Server (e.g., "Customer Last Name is a variable length not null field with a non-unique index..."). Our PDM represents the RDBMS design for an application. We then generate the Data Definition Language (DDL) from the PDM, which we can run within a RDBMS environment to create the set of tables that will store the application's data. To summarize, we go from common business language to business requirements to design to tables.

Although the conceptual, logical, and physical data models have played a very important role in application development over the last 50 years, they will play an even more important role over the next 50 years.

Regardless of the technology, data complexity, or breadth of requirements, there will always be a need for a diagram that captures the business language (conceptual), the business requirements (logical), and the design (physical).

The names *conceptual, logical,* and *physical,* however, are deeply rooted in the RDBMS side. Therefore, we need more encompassing names to accommodate both RDBMS and NoSQL for all three levels.

Align = Conceptual, Refine = Logical, Design = Physical

Using the terms Align, Refine, and Design instead of Conceptual, Logical, and Physical has two benefits: greater purpose and broader context.

Greater purpose means that by rebranding into Align, Refine, and Design, we include what the level does in the name. Align is about agreeing on the common business vocabulary so everyone is *aligned* on terminology and general initiative scope. Refine is about capturing the business requirements. That is, refining our knowledge of the initiative to focus on what is important. Design is about the technical requirements. That is, making sure we accommodate the unique needs of software and hardware on our model.

Broader context means there is more than just the models. When we use terms such as conceptual, most project teams only see the model as the deliverable, and do not recognize all of the work that went into producing the model or other related deliverables such as definitions, issue/question resolutions, and lineage (lineage meaning where the data comes from). The align phase includes the conceptual (business terms) model, the refine phase includes the logical model, and the design phase includes the physical model. We don't lose our modeling terms. Instead, we distinguish the model from its broader phase. For example, instead of saying we are in the logical data modeling phase, we say we are in the refine phase, where the logical data model is one of the deliverables. The logical data model exists within the context of the broader refine phase.

However, if you are working with a group of stakeholders who may not warm up to the traditional names of conceptual, logical, and physical, you can call the conceptual the *alignment model*, the logical the *refinement model*, and the physical the *design model*. Use the terms that would have the largest positive impact on your audience.

The conceptual level is Align, the logical Refine, and the physical Design. Align, Refine, and Design—easy to remember and even rhymes!

Business terms (Align)

We have had many experiences where people who need to speak a common business language do not consistently use the same set of terms. For example, Steve recently facilitated a discussion between a senior business analyst and a senior manager at a large insurance company.

The senior manager expressed his frustration on how a business analyst was slowing down the development of his business analytics application. "The team was meeting with the product owner and business users to complete the user stories on insurance quotes for our upcoming analytics application on quotes, when a business analyst asked the question, *What is a quote?* The rest of the meeting was wasted on trying to answer this question. Why couldn't we just focus on getting the Quote Analytics requirements, which we were in that meeting to do? We are supposed to be Agile!"

If there was a lengthy discussion trying to clarify the meaning of a quote, there is a good chance this insurance company does not understand a quote well. All business users may agree that a quote is an estimate for a policy premium but disagree at what point an estimate becomes a quote. For example, does an estimate have to be based on a certain percentage of facts before it can be considered a quote?

How well will Quote Analytics meet the user requirements if the users are not clear as to what a *quote* is? Imagine needing to know the answer to this question:

How many life insurance quotes were written last quarter in the northeast?

Without a common alignment and understanding of *quote*, one user can answer this question based on their definition of *quote*, and someone else can answer based on their different definition of *quote*. One of these users (or possibly both) will most likely get the wrong answer.

Steve worked with a university whose employees could not agree on what a *student* meant, a manufacturing company whose sales and accounting departments differed on the meaning of *return on total assets*, and a financial company whose analysts battled relentlessly over the meaning of a *trade*—it's all the same challenge we need to overcome, isn't it?

It's about working towards a common business language.

A common business language is a prerequisite for success in any initiative. We can capture and communicate the terms underlying business processes and requirements, enabling people with different backgrounds and roles to understand and communicate with each other.

A Conceptual Data Model (CDM), more appropriately called a Business Terms Model (BTM), is a language of symbols and text that simplifies an informational landscape by providing a precise, minimal, and visual tool scoped for a particular initiative and tailored for a particular audience.

This definition includes the need to be well-scoped, precise, minimal, and visual. Knowing the type of visual that will have the greatest effectiveness requires knowing the audience for the model.

The audience includes the people who will validate and use the model. Validate means telling us whether the model is correct or needs adjustments. Use means reading and benefiting from the model. The scope encompasses an initiative, such as an application development project or a business intelligence program.

Knowing the audience and scope helps us decide which terms to model, what the terms mean, how the terms relate to each other, and the most beneficial type of visual. Additionally, knowing the scope ensures we don't "boil the ocean" and model every possible term in the enterprise. Instead, only focusing on those that will add value to our current initiative.

Although this model is traditionally called a *conceptual data model*, the term "conceptual" is often not received as a very positive term by those outside the data field. "Conceptual" sounds like a term the IT team would come up with. Therefore, we prefer to call the "conceptual data model" the "business terms model" and will use this term going forward. It is about business terms, and including the term "business" raises its importance as a business-focused deliverable and also aligns with data governance.

A business terms model often fits nicely on a single piece of paper—and not a plotter-size paper! Limiting a BTM to one page is important because it encourages us to select only key terms. We can fit 20 terms on one page but not 500 terms.

Being well-scoped, precise, minimal, and visual, the BTM provides a common business language. As a result, we can capture and communicate complex and encompassing business processes and requirements, enabling people with different backgrounds and roles to initially discuss and debate terms, and to eventually communicate effectively using these terms.

With more and more data being created and used, combined with intense competition, strict regulations, and rapid-spread social media, the financial, liability, and credibility stakes have never been higher. Therefore the need for a common business language has never been greater. For example, Figure 22 contains a BTM for our animal shelter.

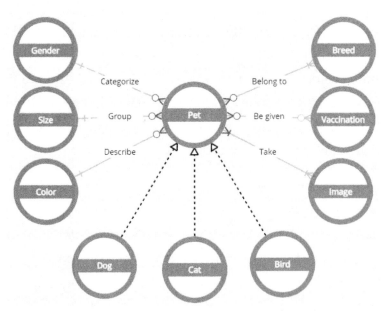

Figure 22: A business terms model for our animal shelter.

Each of these entities will have a precise and clear definition. For example, **Pet** might have a similar definition to what appears in Wikipedia:

A pet, or companion animal, is an animal kept primarily for a person's company or entertainment rather than as a working animal, livestock, or a laboratory animal.

More than likely, though, there will be something about the definition that provides more meaning to the reader of a particular data model and is more specific to a particular initiative, such as:

A pet is a dog, cat, or bird that has passed all the exams required to secure adoption. For example, if Sparky has passed all of his physical and behavioral exams, we would consider Sparky a pet. However, if Sparky has failed at least one exam, we will label Sparky an animal that we will reevaluate later.

Let's now walk through the relationships:

- Each Pet may be either a Dog, Cat, or Bird.
- Dog is a Pet.
- Cat is a Pet.
- Bird is a Pet.
- Each Gender may categorize many Pets.
- Each Pet must be categorized by one Gender.
- Each Size may group many Pets.
- Each Pet must be grouped by one Size.
- Each Color may describe many Pets.
- Each Pet must be described by one Color.
- Each Pet must belong to many Breeds.
- Each Breed may categorize many Pets.
- Each Pet may be given many Vaccinations.

- Each Vaccination may be given to many Pets.
- Each Pet must take many Images.
- Each Image must be taken of many Pets.

Logical (Refine)

A logical data model (LDM) is a business solution to a business problem. It is how the modeler refines the business requirements without complicating the model with implementation concerns such as software and hardware.

For example, after capturing the common business language for a new order application on a BTM, the LDM will refine this model with attributes and more detailed relationships and entities to capture the requirements for this order application. The BTM would contain definitions for **Order** and **Customer**, and the LDM would contain the **Order** and **Customer** attributes needed to deliver the requirements.

Returning to our animal shelter example, Figure 23 contains a subset of the logical data model for our animal shelter.

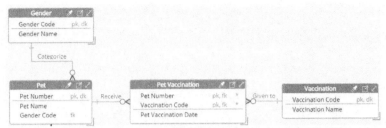

Figure 23: Logical data model subset for our animal shelter.

The requirements for our shelter application appear on this model. This model shows the attributes and relationships needed to deliver a solution to the business. For example, in the **Pet** entity, each **Pet** is identified by a **Pet Number** and described by its name and gender. **Gender** and **Vaccination** are defined lists. We also capture that a **Pet** must have one **Gender** and can receive any number (including zero) of **Vaccinations**.

Note that an LDM in the context of relational databases respects the rules of normalization. Hence in the above diagram, there are associative entities, also known as "junction tables", which prepare for the physical implementation of many-to-many relationships.

Since MongoDB allows us to embed and denormalize, we often don't need these "junction tables" and opt for a simpler view of the same business rules. We can keep together what belongs together, following the Domain-Driven Design concept of "aggregates" discussed below, and leveraging denormalization. See Figure 24.

Figure 24: This denormalized representation can easily lead to a normalized physical data model, whereas the opposite is not necessarily true in more complex configurations.

An important part of the requirements-gathering exercise is to identify, quantify, and qualify the workload by recording frequency of queries, latency of results, volume and velocity of data, retentions, etc. This is discussed in more detail in the Refine chapter.

Domain-Driven Design

It is useful at this stage to briefly cover a popular methodology used in software development: Domain-Driven Design. Its principles have some relevance in the context of data modeling for NoSQL.

Eric Evans is the author of the book, *Domain-Driven Design: Tackling Complexity in the Heart of Software*, published in 2003, which is considered one of the most influential works on Domain-Driven Design (DDD). Its principles include:

- **Ubiquitous language**: establishing a common language used by all stakeholders of a project, and reflecting the concepts and terms that are relevant to the business.

- **Bounded context**: managing the complexity of the system by breaking it down into smaller, more manageable pieces. This is done by defining a boundary around each specific domain of the software system. Each bounded context has its own model and language that is appropriate for that context.

- **Domain model**: using a business terms model of the domain that represents the important entities, their relationships, and the behaviors of the domain.

- **Context mapping**: defining and managing the interactions and relationships between different bounded contexts. Context mapping helps to ensure that different models are consistent with each other and that communication between teams is effective.

- **Aggregates**: identifying clusters of related objects, and treating each of them as a single unit of change. Aggregates help to enforce consistency and integrity within a domain.

- **Continuous refinement**: an iterative process with continuous refinement of the domain model as new insights and requirements are discovered. The domain model should evolve and improve over time based on feedback from stakeholders and users.

These principles are striking by their common sense and are applicable to enhance data modeling. Yet, the nuances are important. For example, we have seen that a BTM helps build a common vocabulary. DDD pushes further for developers to use this language in the code and in the name of collections/tables and fields/columns.

Some data modeling traditionalists have expressed reservations about DDD (and also about Agile development.) For every methodology and technology, there are, of course, examples of misinterpretation and misguided efforts. But applied with clairvoyance and experience, DDD and Agile can lead to great success. We see DDD principles as directly applicable to data modeling to further enhance its relevance, rather than as an opposite approach.

In the context of NoSQL databases and modern architecture patterns and stacks, including event-driven and micro-services, DDD is particularly relevant. Specifically, the DDD concept of "aggregates" matches the hierarchical nature of JSON documents with nested objects and denormalization. As a result, the strict definition of a logical data model is too constraining as it implies that the technology-agnostic model respects the rules of normalization. Hackolade has extended the capabilities of its technology-agnostic models to allow complex data types for nesting and denormalization in Polyglot data models to accommodate the support of NoSQL structures.

Physical (Design)

The physical data model (PDM) is the logical data model compromised for specific software or hardware. The BTM captures our common business vocabulary, the LDM our business requirements, and the PDM our technical requirements. That is, the PDM is a data model of our business requirements structured to work well with our technology. The physical represents the technical design.

While building the PDM, we address the issues that have to do with specific hardware or software, such as, how can we best design our structures to:

- Process this operational data as quickly as possible?
- Make this information secure?
- Answer these business questions with a sub-second response?

For example, Figure 25 contains a relational version and Figure 26 a nested version of a subset of the physical data model for our animal shelter:

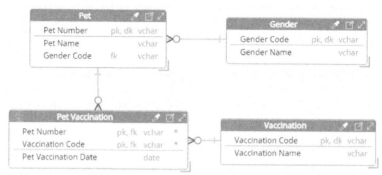

Figure 25: Relational physical data models for our animal shelter.

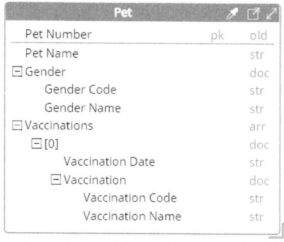

Figure 26: Nested physical data models for our animal shelter.

We have compromised our logical model to work with specific technology. For example, if we are implementing in a RDBMS such as Oracle, we might need to combine (denormalize) structures together to make retrieval performance acceptable.

Figure 25 is a normalized RDBMS model and Figure 26 shows one possible denormalization to leverage the document approach of MongoDB. Information belonging together is kept together with the nesting of subobjects. The cardinality of the relational junction table Pet Vaccination is replaced by an array to store multiple Vaccinations. This aggregation approach enables the referential integrity of the atomic unit of each document. Note that the nesting does not prevent the existence of a Vaccination table if an access pattern in the application requires it, but would then require synchronization of the denormalized data to ensure consistency.

Three model perspectives

Relational Database Management System (RDBMS) and NoSQL are the two main modeling perspectives. Within the RDBMS, the two settings are relational and dimensional. Within NoSQL, the one setting is query. Therefore, the three modeling perspectives are relational, dimensional, and query.

Table 3 contrasts relational, dimensional, and query. In this section, we will go into more detail into each of these perspectives.

Factor	Relational	Dimensional	Query
Benefit	Precisely representing data through sets	Precisely representing how data will be analyzed	Precisely representing how data will be received and accessed
Focus	Business rules _constraining_ a business process	Business questions _analyzing_ a business process	Access paths _providing_ _insights_ into a business process
Use case	Operational (OLTP)	Analytics (OLAP)	Discovery
Parent perspective	RDBMS	RDBMS	NoSQL
Example	A Customer must own at least one Account.	How much revenue did we generate in fees by Date, Region, and Product? Also want to see by Month and Year...	Which customers own a checking account that generated over $10,000 in fees this year, own at least one cat, and live within 500 miles of New York City?

Table 3: Comparing relational, dimensional, and query.

A RDBMS stores data in sets based on Ted Codd's groundbreaking white papers written from 1969 through 1974. Codd's ideas were implemented in the RDBMS with tables (entities at the physical level) containing attributes.

Each table has a primary key and foreign key constraints to enforce the relationships between tables. The RDBMS has been around for so many years primarily because of its ability to retain data integrity by enforcing rules that maintain high-quality data. Secondly, the RDBMS enables efficiency in storing data, reducing redundancy, and saving storage space at the cost of using more CPU power. Over the last decade, the benefit of saving space has diminished as disks get cheaper while CPU performance is not improving. Both trajectories favor NoSQL databases these days.

NoSQL means "NoRDBMS". A NoSQL database stores data differently than a RDBMS. A RDBMS stores data in tables (sets) where primary and foreign keys drive data integrity and navigation. A NoSQL database does not store data in sets. For example, MongoDB stores data in BSON format. Other NoSQL solutions may store data in Resource Description Framework (RDF) triplesExtensible Markup Language (XML), or JavaScript Object Notation (JSON).

Relational, dimensional, and query can exist at all three model levels, giving us nine different types of models, as shown in Table 4. We discussed the three levels of Align, Refine, and Design in the previous section. We align on a common business language, refine our business requirements, and then design our database. For example, if we are modeling a new claims application for an insurance company, we might create a relational model capturing the business rules within the claims process. The BTM would capture the claims business vocabulary, the LDM would capture the claims business requirements, and the PDM would capture the claims database design.

	RELATIONAL	DIMENSIONAL	NoSQL
BUSINESS TERMS (ALIGN)	TERMS AND RULES	TERMS AND PATHS	TERMS AND QUERIES
LOGICAL (REFINE)	SETS	MEASURES WITH CONTEXT	QUERY-FOCUSED HIERACHY
PHYSICAL (DESIGN)	COMPROMISED SETS	STAR SCHEMA OR SNOWFLAKE	ENHANCED HIERACHY

Table 4: Nine different types of models.

Relational

Relational models work best when there is a requirement to capture and enforce business rules. For example, a relational model may be ideal if an operational application requires applying many business rules, such as an order application ensuring that every order line belongs to one and only one order, and that each order line is identified by its order number plus a sequence number. The relational perspective focuses on business rules.

We can build a relational at all three levels: business terms, logical, and physical. The relational business terms model contains the common business language for a particular initiative. Relationships capture the business rules between these terms. The relational logical data model includes entities along with their definitions, relationships, and attributes. The relational physical data model includes physical structures such as tables, columns, and constraints. The business terms, logical, and physical data models shared earlier are examples of relational. See Figure 27, Figure 28, and Figure 29.

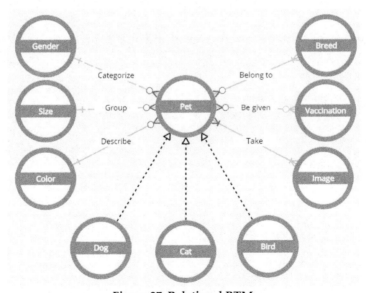

Figure 27: Relational BTM.

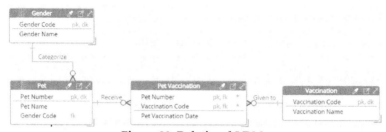

Figure 28: Relational LDM.

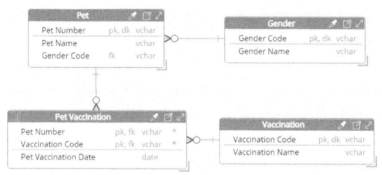

Figure 29: Relational PDM.

Figure 30 contains another example of a BTM.

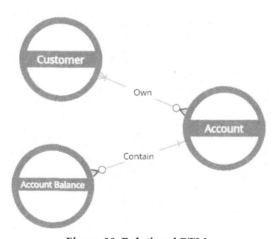

Figure 30: Relational BTM.

The relationships capture that:

- Each **Customer** may own many **Accounts**.
- Each **Account** must be owned by many **Customers**.
- Each **Account** may contain many **Account Balances**.
- Each **Account Balance** must belong to one **Account**.

We wrote the following definitions during one of our meetings with the project sponsor:

Customer	A customer is a person or organization who has opened one or more accounts with our bank. If members of a household each have their own account, each member of a household is considered a distinct customer. If someone has opened an account and then closed it, they are still considered a customer.
Account	An account is a contractual arrangement by which our bank holds funds on behalf of a customer.
Account Balance	An account balance is a financial record of how much money a customer has in a particular account with our bank at the end of a given time period, such as someone's checking account balance at the end of a month.

For the relational logical data model, we assign attributes to entities (sets) using a set of rules called *normalization*.

Although normalization has a foundation in mathematics (set theory and predicate calculus), we see it more as a technique to design a flexible structure. More specifically, we define normalization as a process of asking business questions, increasing your knowledge of the business and enabling you to build flexible structures that support high-quality data.

The business questions are organized around levels, including First Normal Form (1NF), Second Normal Form (2NF), and Third Normal Form (3NF). These three levels have been neatly summarized by William Kent:

Every attribute depends upon the key, the whole key, and nothing but the key, so help me Codd.

"Every attribute depends upon the key" is 1NF, "the whole key" is 2NF, and "nothing but the key" is 3NF. Note that the higher levels of normalization include the lower levels, so 2NF includes 1NF, and 3NF includes 2NF and 1NF.

To make sure that every attribute depends upon the key (1NF), we need to make sure for a given primary key value, we get at most one value back from each attribute. For example, **Author Name** assigned to a **Book** entity would violate 1NF because for a given book, such as this book, we can have more than author. Therefore **Author Name** does not belong to the **Book** set (entity) and needs to be moved to a different entity. More than likely, **Author Name** will be assigned to the **Author** entity, and a relationship will exist between **Book** and **Author**, stating among other things, that a **Book** can be written by more than one **Author**.

To make sure every attribute depends upon the whole key (2NF), we need to make sure we have the minimal primary key. For example, if the primary key for **Book** was both **ISBN** and a **Book Title**, we would quickly learn that **Book Title** is not necessary to have in the primary key. An attribute such as **Book Price** would depend directly on the **ISBN,** and therefore including **Book Title** in the primary key would not add any value.

To make sure there are no hidden dependencies ("nothing but the key," which is 3NF), we need to make sure every attribute depends directly on the primary key and nothing else. For example, the attribute **Order Gross Amount** does not depend directly on the primary key of **Order** (most likely, **Order Number**). Instead, **Order Gross Amount** depends upon **List Price** and **Item Quantity,** which are used to derive the **Order Gross Amount**.

Data Modeling Made Simple, by Steve Hoberman, goes more into detail into each of the levels of normalization, including the levels above 3NF. Realize the main purpose of normalization is to correctly organize attributes into sets. Also, note that the normalized model is built according to the properties of the data and not built according to how the data is being used.

Dimensional models are built to answer specific business questions with ease, and NoSQL models are built to answer queries and identify patterns with ease. The relational model is the only model focused on the intrinsic properties of the data and not usage.

Dimensional

A dimensional data model captures the business *questions* behind one or more business processes. The answers to the questions are metrics, such as **Gross Sales Amount** and **Customer Count**.

A dimensional model is a data model whose only purpose is to allow efficient and user-friendly filtering, sorting, and summing of measures. That is, analytics applications. The relationships on a dimensional model represent navigation paths instead of business rules, as with the relational model. The scope of a dimensional model is a collection of related measures plus context that together address some business process. We build dimensional models based upon one or more business questions that evaluate a business process. We parse the business questions into measures and ways of looking at these measures to create the model.

For example, suppose we work for a bank and would like to better understand the fee generation process. In that case, we might ask the business question, "What is the total amount of fees received by **Account Type** (such as Checking or Savings), **Month, Customer Category** (such as Individual or Corporate), and **Branch**?" See Figure 31. This model also communicates the requirement to see fees not just at a **Month** level but also at a **Year** level, not just a **Branch** level, but also at a **Region** and **District** level.

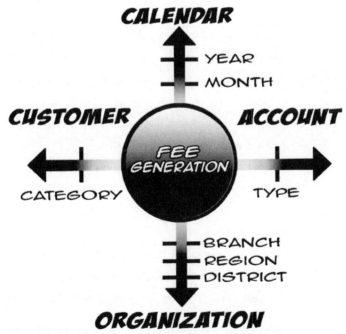

Figure 31: A dimensional BTM for a bank.

Term definitions:

Fee Generation	Fee generation is the business process where money is charged to customers for the privilege to conduct transactions against their account, or money charged based on time intervals, such as monthly charges to keep a checking account open that has a low balance.
Branch	A branch is a physical location open for business. Customers visit branches to conduct transactions.
Region	A region is our bank's own definition of dividing a country into smaller pieces for branch assignment or reporting purposes.
District	A district is a grouping of regions used for organizational assignments or reporting purposes. Districts can and often do cross country boundaries, such as North America and Europe districts.
Customer Category	A customer category is a grouping of one or more customers for reporting or organizational purposes. Examples of customer categories are Individual, Corporate, and Joint.
Account Type	An account type is a grouping of one or more accounts for reporting or organizational purposes. Examples of account types are Checking, Savings, and Brokerage.
Year	A year is a period of time containing 365 days, consistent with the Gregorian calendar.
Month	A month is each of the twelve named periods into which a year is divided.

You might encounter terms such as **Year** and **Month** which are commonly understood terms, and therefore minimal time can be invested in writing a definition. Make sure, though, that these are commonly understood terms, as sometimes even **Year** can have multiple meanings, such as whether the reference is to a fiscal or standard calendar.

Fee Generation is an example of a meter. A meter represents the business process that we need to measure. The meter is so important to the dimensional model that the name of the meter is often the name of the application: the **Sales** meter, the Sales Analytics Application. **District, Region**, and **Branch** represent the levels of detail we can navigate within the **Organization** dimension. A *dimension* is a subject whose purpose is to add meaning to the measures. For example, **Year** and **Month** represent the levels of detail we can navigate within the **Calendar** dimension. So this model contains four dimensions: **Organization**, **Calendar**, **Customer**, and **Account**.

Suppose an organization builds an analytical application to answer questions on how a business process is performing, such as a sales analytics application. Business questions become very important in this case, so we build a dimensional data model. The dimensional perspective focuses on business questions. We can build a dimensional data model at all three levels: business terms, logical, and physical. Figure 31 displayed our business terms model, Figure 32 shows the logical, and Figure 33 the physical.

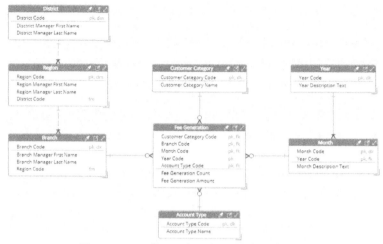

Figure 32: A dimensional LDM for a bank.

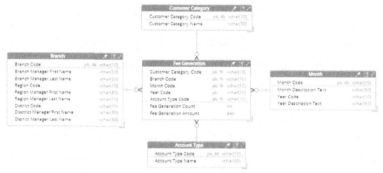

Figure 33: A dimensional PDM for a bank.

Query

Suppose an organization builds an application to discover something new about a business process, such as a fraud detection application. Queries become very important in that case, so we build a query data model.

We can build a query data model at all three levels: business terms, logical, and physical. Figure 34 contains a query business terms model, Figure 35 and Figure 36 the query logical data models, and Figure 37 the query physical data model.

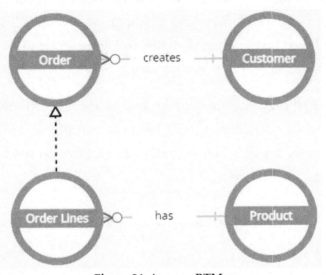

Figure 34: A query BTM.

The Query BTM does not look any different from other BTMs as the vocabulary and scope are the same, independent of the physical database implementation. In fact, we can even ask the Participation and Existence questions for each relationship in our query BTM, if we feel that it would add value. In the above example:

- a **Customer** creates an **Order**
- an **Order** is made of **Order Lines**
- an **Order Line** has a **Product**

It is possible to toggle the display of attributes for the different entities.

When it comes to the logical model, however, access patterns and workload analysis dictate the model. Depending on whether there are queries for maintenance screens for Customers and Products, you could have the strictly embedded logical model in Figure 35, or the model in Figure 36.

The first logical model would lead to a single collection in MongoDB, whereas it will be automatically normalized into three tables when instantiated to a physical model for a relational database.

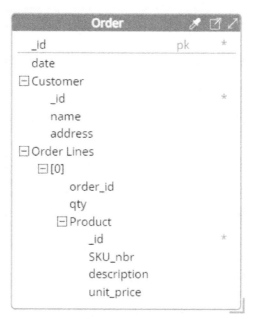

Figure 35: Strictly embedded logical model.

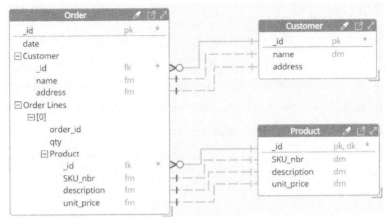

Figure 36: A query LDM.

The second logical model will lead to three collections in MongoDB to accommodate the maintenance of **Customers** and **Products**, but keeping the **Order** table as an aggregate combines embedding and referencing schema design patterns.

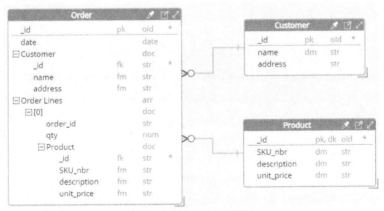

Figure 37: A query PDM.

In the above model, we show nesting, denormalization, and referencing. Nesting allows aggregating information that belongs together in a user-friendly structure to make it easily understandable by humans. Denormalization is implemented so a query to retrieve an order would fetch all of the necessary information in a single seek, without having to execute expensive joins, even if it is a repetition of the data in the master collections Customer and Product. There might still be access patterns required to view and update Customer information and Product information regardless of the orders to which they might be linked. Therefore, we keep the master Customer collection and the master Product collection. In the Order collection, we keep a reference to the master document. Since there is no cross-document referential integrity built into the database engine, the responsibility to maintain the synchronization shifts to the application or to an offline process such as a Kafka pub/sub pipeline.

One final remark: there could be a good reason to not update a denormalized piece of information. For example, the ship-to address of an already fulfilled order should not be updated because a customer moves to a new address. Only pending orders should be updated. Denormalization is sometimes more precise than cascading updates.

CHAPTER 1

Align

This chapter will explain the data modeling align phase. We explain the purpose of aligning our business vocabulary, introduce our animal shelter case study, and then walk through the align approach. We end this chapter with three tips and three takeaways.

Purpose

The align stage aims to capture a common business vocabulary within a business terms model for a particular initiative.

For NoSQL models, you might use a different term than a business terms model, such as a *query alignment model*. We also like this term, which is more specific to the purpose of a NoSQL BTM, as our goal is modeling the queries.

Our animal shelter

A small animal shelter needs our help. They currently advertise their ready-to-adopt pets on their own website. They use a Microsoft Access relational database to keep track of their animals, and they publish this data weekly on their website. See Figure 38 for their current process.

A Microsoft Access record is created for each animal after the animal passes a series of intake tests and is deemed ready for adoption. The animal is called a pet once they are ready for adoption.

Once a week, the pet records are updated on the shelter's website. New pets are added and adopted pets have been removed.

Figure 38: Animal shelter current architecture.

Not many people know about this shelter, and, therefore, animals often remain unadopted for much longer than the national average. Consequently, they would like to partner with a group of animal shelters to form a consortium where all of the shelters' pet information will appear on a much more popular website. Our shelter will need to extract data from its current MS Access database and send it to the consortium database in JSON format. The consortium will then load these JSON feeds into their MongoDB database with a web front end.

Let's now look at the shelter's current models.

The animal shelter built the business terms model (BTM) in Figure 39 to capture the common business language for the initiative.

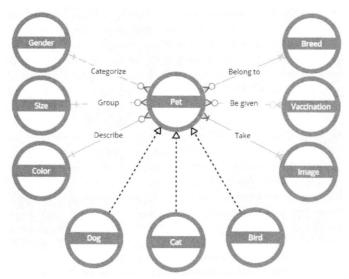

Figure 39: Animal shelter BTM.

In addition to this diagram, the BTM also contains precise definitions for each term, such as this definition **Pet** mentioned earlier in the chapter:

A pet is a dog, cat, or bird that has passed all the exams required to secure adoption. For example, if Sparky has passed all of his physical and behavioral exams, we would consider Sparky a pet. However, if Sparky has failed at least one exam, we will label Sparky an animal that we will reevaluate later.

Our animal shelter knows its world well and has built fairly solid models. Recall they will send a subset of their data to a consortium via JSON, which the consortium's MongoDB database will receive and load for display on their website. Let's go through the align, refine, and design approach for the consortium, and then work on the JSON structure required to move the shelter's data from Microsoft Access to MongoDB.

Approach

The align stage is about developing the initiative's common business vocabulary. We will follow the steps shown in Figure 40.

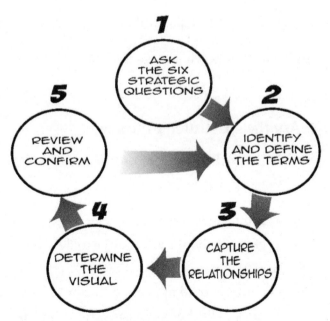

Figure 40: Steps to create a BTM.

Before you begin any project, we must ask six strategic questions (Step 1). These questions are a prerequisite to the success of any initiative because they ensure we choose the right terms for our BTM. Next, identify all terms within the scope of the initiative (Step 2). Make sure each term is clearly and completely defined. Then determine how these terms are related to each other (Step 3). Often, you will need to go back to Step 2 at this point because in capturing relationships, you may come up with new terms. Next, determine the most beneficial visual for your audience (Step 4). Consider the visual that would resonate best with those that will need to review and use your BTM. As a final step, seek approval of your BTM (Step 5). Often at this point, there are additional changes to the model, and we cycle through these steps until the model is accepted.

Let's build a BTM following these five steps.

Step 1: Ask the six strategic questions

Six questions must be asked to ensure a valuable BTM. These questions appear in Figure 41.

1. **What is our initiative?** This question ensures we know enough about the initiative to determine the scope. Knowing the scope allows us to decide which terms should appear on the initiative's BTM. Eric Evans, in his book *Domain-Driven Design*,

introduces the concept of "Bounded Context," which is all about understanding and defining your scope. For example, terms such as **Animal, Shelter Employee**, and **Pet Food** are out of scope.

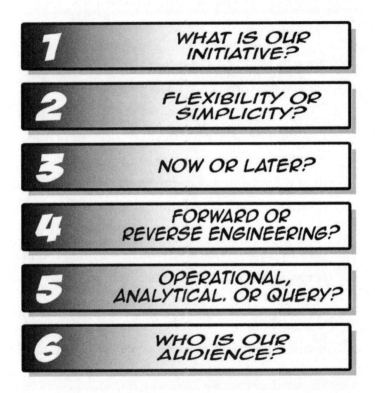

Figure 41: Six questions to ensure model success.

2. **Flexibility or simplicity?** This question ensures we introduce generic terms only if there is a need for flexibility. Generic terms allow us to accommodate new types of terms that we do not know about today and also allow us to better group similar terms together. For example, **Person** is flexible and

Employee is simple. **Person** can include other terms we have not yet considered, such as **Adopter, Veterinarian**, and **Volunteer**. However, **Person** can be a more difficult term to relate to than **Employee**. We often describe our processes using business-specific terms like **Employee**.

3. **Now or later?** This question ensures we have chosen the correct time perspective for our BTM. BTMs capture a common business language at a point in time. If we are intent on capturing how business processes work or are analyzed today, then we need to make sure terms, along with their definitions and relationships, reflect a current perspective (now). If we are intent on capturing how business processes work or are analyzed at some point in the future, such as one year or three years into the future, then we need to make sure terms, along with their definitions and relationships, reflect a future perspective (later).

4. **Forward or reverse engineering?** This question ensures we select the most appropriate "language" for the BTM. If business requirements drive the initiative, then it is a forward engineering effort and we choose a business language. It does not matter whether the organization is using SAP or Siebel, the BTM will contain business terms. If an application is driving the initiative, then it is a

reverse engineering effort and we choose an application language. If the application uses the term **Object** for the term **Product**, it will appear as **Object** on the model and be defined according to how the application defines the term, not how the business defines the term. As another example of reverse engineering, you might have as your starting point some type of physical data structure, such as a database layout, an XML, or JSON document. For example, the following JSON snippet might reveal the importance of **Shelter Volunteer** as a business term:

```
{
  "name": "John Smith",
  "age": 35,
  "address": {
    "street": "123 Main St",
    "city": "Anytown",
    "state": "CA",
    "zip": "12345"
  }
}
```

5. **Operational, analytics, or query?** This question ensures we choose the right type of BTM—relational, dimensional, or query. Each initiative requires its respective BTM.

6. **Who is our audience?** We need to know who will review our model (validator) and who will use our model going forward (users).

1. *What is our initiative?*

Mary is the animal shelter volunteer responsible for intake. Intake is the process of receiving an animal and preparing the animal for adoption. She has been a volunteer for over ten years, and was the main business resource in building the original Microsoft Access database.

She is enthusiastic about the new initiative, seeing it as a way to get animals adopted in less time. We might start off by interviewing Mary, where the goal is to have a clear understanding of the initiative, including its scope:

> **You**: Thanks for making time to meet with me. This is just our first meeting, and I don't want to keep you behind our allocated time, so let's get right to the purpose of our interview and then a few questions. The earlier we identify our scope and then define the terms within this scope, the greater the chance for success. Can you please share with me more about this initiative?

> **Mary**: Sure! The main driver for our initiative is to make our furry friends get adopted faster. Today on average, our pets are adopted in two weeks. We and other small local shelters would like to get this down to five days on average. Maybe even less, hope so. We will send our pet data to a consortium we have formed with other local shelters to centralize our listings and reach a wider audience.

> **You**: Do you have all types of pets, or just dogs and cats?

Mary: I'm not sure what kinds of pets the other shelters have other than dogs and cats, but we also have birds up for adoption.

You: Ok, and are there any pets to exclude from this initiative?

Mary: Well, it takes a few days for an animal to be assessed to be considered ready for adoption. We run some tests and sometimes procedures. I like to use the term pet when an animal has completed these processes and is now ready for adoption. So we do have animals that are not yet pets. We are only including pets in this initiative.

You: Got it. And when somebody is looking for a furry best friend, what kinds of filters would they use?

Mary: I've talked with volunteers at the other shelters too. We feel after filtering first on the type of pet, such as dog, cat, or bird, filtering by breed, gender, color, and size would be the most important filters.

You: What kinds of information would someone expect to see when clicking on a pet description that was returned by the filter selections?

Mary: Lots of images, a cute name, maybe information on the pet's color or breed. That sort of thing.

You: Makes sense. What about people? Do you care about people as part of this initiative?

Mary: What do you mean?

You: Well, the people who drop off pets and the people who adopt pets.

Mary: Yes, yes. We keep track of this information. By the way, the people who drop off animals we call surrenderers, and the people who adopt pets are adopters. We are not sending any person details to the consortium. We don't see it relevant and don't want to risk getting sued over privacy issues. Spot the dog will never sue us, but Bob the surrenderer might.

You: I can understand that. Well, I think I understand the scope of the initiative, thank you.

We now have a good understanding of the scope of the initiative. It includes all pets (not all animals) and no people. As we refine the terminology, we might have more questions for Mary around scope.

2. Flexibility or simplicity?

Let's continue the interview to answer the next question.

You: Flexibility or simplicity?

Mary: I don't understand the question.

You: We need to determine whether to use generic terms or, for lack of a better word, more concrete terms. Using generic terms, such as mammal instead of **dog** or **cat,** allows us to accommodate future terms later, such as other kinds of mammals like monkeys or whales.

Mary: We haven't had many whales up for adoption this month. [laughs]

You: Ha!

Mary: Flexibility sounds appealing, but we shouldn't go overboard. I can see eventually we might have other kinds of pets, so a certain level of flexibility would be useful here. But not too much. I remember working on the Microsoft Access system and someone was trying to get us to use a Party concept to capture dogs and cats. It was too hard for us to get our heads around it. Too fuzzy, if you know what I mean.

You: I do know what you mean. Ok, a little flexibility to accommodate different kinds of pets, but not to go overboard. Got it.

3. Now or later?

Now on to the next question.

You: Should our model reflect how things are now at the shelter or how you would like it to be after the consortium's application is live?

Mary: I don't think it matters. We are not changing anything with the new system. A pet is a pet.

You: Ok, that makes things easy.

As we can see from our conversations on these first three questions, getting to the answers is rarely straightforward and easy. However, it is much more efficient to ask them at the beginning of the initiative instead of making assumptions early on and having to perform rework later, when changes are time-consuming and expensive.

4. Forward or reverse engineering?

Since we first need to understand how the business works before implementing a software solution, this is a forward engineering project, and we will choose the forward engineering option. This means driven by requirements and, therefore, our terms will be business terms instead of application terms.

5. Operational, analytics, or query?

Since this initiative is about displaying pet information to drive pet adoption, which is query, we will build a query BTM.

6. Who is our audience?

That is, who is going to validate the model and who is going to use it going forward? Mary seems like the best candidate to be the validator. She knows the existing application and processes very well and is vested in ensuring the new initiative succeeds. Potential adopters will be the users of the system.

Step 2: Identify and define the terms

We first focus on the user stories, then determine the detailed queries for each story, and finally sequence these queries in the order they occur. It can be iterative. For example, we might identify the sequence between two queries and realize that a query in the middle is missing that will require modifying or adding a user story. Let's go through each of these three steps.

1. Write user stories

User stories have been around for a long time and are extremely useful for NoSQL modeling. Wikipedia defines a user story as: ...*an informal, natural language description of features of a software system.*

The user story provides the scope and overview for the BTM, also known as a query alignment model. A query alignment model accommodates one or more user stories. The purpose of a user story is to capture at a very high level how an initiative will deliver business value. User stories take the structure of the template in Figure 42.

TEMPLATE	COVERS
AS A (STAKEHOLDER)	WHO?
I WANT TO (REQUIREMENT)	WHAT?
SO THAT (MOTIVATION)	WHY?

Figure 42: User story template.

Here are some examples of user stories from tech.gsa.gov:

- As a Content Owner, I want to be able to create product content so that I can provide information and market to customers.

- As an Editor, I want to review content before it is published so that I can ensure it is optimized with correct grammar and tone.

- As a HR Manager, I need to view a candidate's status so that I can manage their application process throughout the recruiting phases.

- As a Marketing Data Analyst, I need to run the Salesforce and Google analytics reports so that I can build the monthly media campaign plans.

To keep our animal shelter example relatively simple, assume our animal shelter and others that are part of the consortium met and determined these are the most popular user stories:

1. As a potential dog adopter, I want to find a particular breed, color, size, and gender, so that I get the type of dog I am looking. I want to ensure that the dog's vaccinations are up-to-date.

2. As a potential bird adopter, I want to find a particular breed and color so that I get the bird I am looking for.

3. As a potential cat adopter, I want to find a particular color and gender, so that I get the type of cat I am looking for.

2. Capture queries

Next, we capture the queries for the one or more user stories within our initiative's scope. While we want to capture multiple user stories to ensure we have a firm grasp of the scope, having just a single user story that drives a NoSQL application is ok. A query starts off with a "verb" and is an action to do something. Some NoSQL database vendors use the phrase "access pattern" instead of query. We will use the term "query" to also encompass "access pattern".

Here are the queries that satisfy our three user stories:

Q1: Only show pets available for adoption.

Q2: Search available dogs by breed, color, size, and gender that have up-to-date vaccinations.

Q3: Search available birds by breed and color.

Q4: Search available cats by color and gender.

Now that we have direction, we can work with the business experts to identify and define the terms within the initiative's scope.

Recall our definition of a term as a noun that represents a collection of business data and is considered both basic and critical to your audience for a particular initiative. A term can fit into one of six categories: who, what, when, where, why, or how. We can use these six categories to create a terms template for capturing the terms on our BTM. See Figure 43.

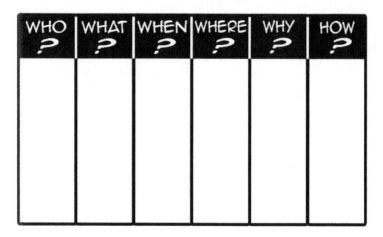

Figure 43: Terms template.

This is a handy brainstorming tool. There is no significance to the numbers. That is, a term written next to #1 is not meant to be more important than a term written next to #2. In addition, you can have more than five terms in a given column, or in some cases, no terms in a given column.

We meet again with Mary, and came up with this completed template in Figure 44, based on our queries.

WHO ?	WHAT ?	WHEN ?	WHERE ?	WHY ?	HOW ?
SURRENDERER	PET	VACCINATION DATE	CRATE	VACCINATE	VACCINATION
ADOPTER	DOG			ADOPT	ADOPTION
	CAT			PROMOTE	PROMOTION
	BIRD				
	BREED				
	GENDER				
	COLOR				
	SIZE				
	IMAGE				

Figure 44: Initially completed template for our animal shelter.

Notice that this is a brainstorming session, and terms might appear on this template but not on the relational BTM. Excluded terms fit into three categories:

- **Too detailed**. Attributes will appear on the LDM and not the BTM. For example, **Vaccination Date** is more detailed than **Pet** and **Breed**.

- **Out of scope**. Brainstorming is a great way to test the scope of the initiative. Often, terms added to the terms template require additional discussions to determine whether they are in scope. For example, **Surrenderer** and **Adopter** we know are out of scope for the animal shelter's initiative.

- **Redundancies**. Why and How can be very similar. For example, the event **Vaccinate** is documented by the **Vaccination**. The event **Adopt** is documented by **Adoption**. Therefore, we may not need both the event and documentation. In this case, we choose the documentation. That is, we choose How instead of Why.

After taking a lunch break, we met again with Mary and refined our terms template, as shown in Figure 45.

WHO ?	WHAT ?	WHEN ?	WHERE ?	WHY ?	HOW ?
~~SURRENDERER~~	PET	~~VACCINATION DATE~~	~~CRATE~~	~~VACCINATE~~	VACCINATION
~~ADOPTER~~	DOG			~~ADOPT~~	~~ADOPTION~~
	CAT			~~PROMOTE~~	~~PROMOTION~~
	BIRD				
	BREED				
	GENDER				
	COLOR				
	SIZE				
	IMAGE				

Figure 45: Refined template for our animal shelter.

We might have a lot of questions during this brainstorming session. It is a great idea to ask questions as they come up. There are three benefits of raising questions:

- **Become known as the detective**. Become comfortable with the level of detective work needed to arrive at a precise set of terms. Look for holes in the definition where ambiguity can sneak in, and ask questions the answers to which will make the definition precise. Consider the question, "Can a pet be of more than one breed?" The answer to this question will refine how the consortium views pets, breeds, and their relationship. A skilled detective remains pragmatic as well, careful to avoid "analysis paralysis". A skilled data modeler must also be pragmatic to ensure the delivery of value to the project team.

- **Uncover hidden terms**. Often the answers to questions lead to more terms on our BTM—terms that we might have missed otherwise. For example, better understanding the relationship between **Vaccination** and **Pet** might lead to more terms on our BTM.

- **Better now than later**. The resulting BTM offers a lot of value, yet the process of getting to that final model is also valuable. Debates and questions challenge people, make them rethink and, in some cases, defend their perspectives. If questions are not raised and answered during the process of building the BTM, the questions will be raised and need to be addressed later on in the lifecycle of the initiative, often in the form of data and process surprises, when changes are time-consuming and expensive. Even simple questions like "Are there other attributes that we could use to describe a pet?" can lead to a healthy debate resulting in a more precise BTM.

Here are definitions for each term:

Pet	A dog, cat, or bird that is ready and available to be adopted. An animal becomes a pet after they have passed certain exams administered by our shelter staff.
Gender	The biological sex of the pet. There are three values that we use at the shelter: • Male • Female • Unknown The unknown value is when we are unsure of the gender.
Size	The size is most relevant for dogs, and there are three values that we assign at the shelter: • Small • Medium • Large Cats and birds are assigned medium, except for kittens which are assigned small and parrots which are large.
Color	The primary shade of the pet's fur, feathers, or coat. Examples of colors include brown, red, gold, cream, and black. If a pet has multiple colors, we either assign a primary color or assign a more general term to encompass multiple colors, such as textured, spotted, or patched.

Breed	From Wikipedia, because this definition applies to our initiative: *A breed is a specific group of domestic animals having homogeneous appearance, homogeneous behavior, and/or other characteristics that distinguish it from other organisms of the same species.*
Vaccina -tion	A shot given to a pet to protect it from disease. Examples of vaccinations are rabies for dogs and cats, and polyomavirus vaccine for birds.
Image	A photograph taken of the pet that will be posted on the website.
Dog	From Wikipedia, because this definition applies to our initiative: *The dog is a domesticated descendant of the wolf. Also called the domestic dog, it is derived from the extinct Pleistocene wolf, and the modern wolf is the dog's nearest living relative. Dogs were the first species to be domesticated by hunter-gatherers over 15,000 years ago before the development of agriculture.*
Cat	From Wikipedia, because this definition applies to our initiative: *The cat is a domestic species of small carnivorous mammal. It is the only domesticated species in the family Felidae and is commonly referred to as the domestic cat or house cat to distinguish it from the wild members of the family.*
Bird	From Wikipedia, because this definition applies to our initiative: *Birds are a group of warm-blooded vertebrates constituting the class Aves, characterized by feathers, toothless beaked jaws, the laying of hard-shelled eggs, a high metabolic rate, a four-chambered heart, and a strong yet lightweight skeleton.*

Step 3: Capture the relationships

Even though this is a query BTM, we can ask the Participation and Existence questions to precisely display the business rules for each relationship. Participation questions determine whether there is a one or a many symbol on the relationship line next to each term. Existence questions determine whether there is a zero (may) or one (must) symbol on the relationship line next to either term.

Working with Mary, we identify these relationships on the model:

- **Pet** can be a **Bird, Cat,** or **Dog.** (Subtyping)
- **Pet** and **Image.**
- **Pet** and **Breed.**
- **Pet** and **Gender.**
- **Pet** and **Color.**
- **Pet** and **Vaccination.**
- **Pet** and **Size.**

Table 5 contains the answers to the Participation and Existence questions for each of these seven relationships (excluding the subtyping relationship).

After translating the answer to each question into the model, we have the animal shelter BTM in Figure 46.

Question	Yes	No
Can a Gender categorize more than one Pet?	✓	
Can a Pet be categorized by more than one Gender?		✓
Can a Gender exist without a Pet?	✓	
Can a Pet exist without a Gender?		✓
Can a Size categorize more than one Pet?	✓	
Can a Pet be categorized by more than one Size?		✓
Can a Size exist without a Pet?	✓	
Can a Pet exist without a Size?		✓
Can a Color describe more than one Pet?	✓	
Can a Pet be described by more than one Color?		✓
Can a Color exist without a Pet?	✓	
Can a Pet exist without a Color?		✓
Can a Pet be described by more than one Breed?	✓	
Can a Breed describe more than one Pet?	✓	
Can a Pet exist without a Breed?		✓
Can a Breed exist without a Pet?	✓	
Can a Pet be given more than one Vaccination?	✓	
Can a Vaccination be given to more than one Pet?	✓	
Can a Pet exist without a Vaccination?	✓	
Can a Vaccination exist without a Pet?	✓	
Can a Pet take more than one Image?	✓	
Can an Image be taken of more than one Pet?	✓	
Can a Pet exist without an Image?		✓
Can an Image exist without a Pet?		✓

Table 5: Answers to the Participation and Existence questions.

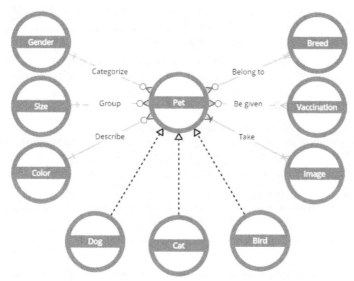

Figure 46: Our animal shelter BTM (showing rules).

These relationships are read as:

- Each **Gender** may categorize many **Pets**.
- Each **Pet** must be categorized by one **Gender**.
- Each **Size** may group many **Pets**.
- Each **Pet** must be grouped by one **Size**.
- Each **Color** may describe many **Pets**.
- Each **Pet** must be described by one **Color**.
- Each **Pet** must belong to many **Breeds**.
- Each **Breed** may be assigned to many **Pets**.
- Each **Pet** may be given many **Vaccinations**.
- Each **Vaccination** may be given to many **Pets**.
- Each **Pet** must take many **Images**.
- Each **Image** must be taken of many **Pets**.
- Each **Pet** may either be a **Dog**, **Cat**, or **Bird**.
- **Dog** is a **Pet**. **Cat** is a **Pet**. **Bird** is a **Pet**.

The answers to the participation and existence questions are context-dependent. That is, the scope of the initiative determines the answers. In this case, because our scope is the subset of the animal shelter's business that will be used as part of this consortium's project, we know at this point that a **Pet** must be described by only one **Color**.

We determined, though, that a MongoDB database should be used to answer these queries. You can see how the traditional data model provides value in terms of making us ask the right questions and then providing a powerful communication medium showing the terms and their business rules. Even if we are not implementing our solution in a relational database, this BTM provides value.

Build a relational data model even though the solution is in a NoSQL database such as MongoDB, if you feel there can be value. That is, if you feel there is value in explaining the terms with precision along with their business rules, build the relational BTM. If you feel there is value in organizing the attributes into sets using normalization, build the relational LDM. It will help you organize your thoughts and provide you with a very effective communication tool.

Our end goal, though, is to create a MongoDB database. Therefore, we need a query BTM. So we need to determine the order in which someone would run the queries.

Graphing the sequence of queries leads to the query BTM. The query BTM is a numbered list of all queries necessary to deliver the user stories within the initiative's scope. The model also shows a sequence or dependency among the queries. The query BTM for our five queries would look like what appears in Figure 47.

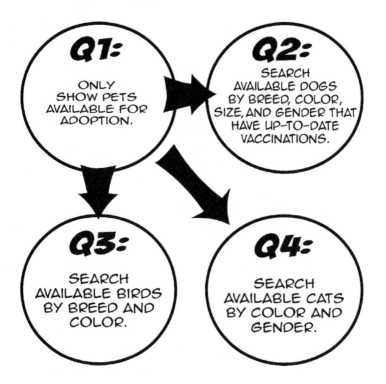

Figure 47: Our animal shelter BTM (showing queries).

All of the queries depend on the first query. That is, we first need to filter by animal type.

Step 4: Determine the visual

Someone will need to review your work and use your model as input for future deliverables such as software development, so deciding on the most useful visual is an important step. After getting an answer to Strategic Question #4, *Who is our audience?*, we know that Mary will be our validator.

There are many different ways of displaying the BTM. Factors include the technical competence of the audience and the existing tools environment.

However, it would be helpful to know which data modeling notations and data modeling tools are currently being used within the organization. If the audience is familiar with a particular data modeling notation—such as Information Engineering (IE), which we have been using throughout this book—that is the notation we should use. If the audience is familiar with a particular data modeling tool, such as IDERA's ER/Studio, erwin DM, or Hackolade Studio, and that data modeling tool uses a different notation, we should use that tool with that notation to create the BTM.

Luckily, the two BTMs we created, one for rules and one for queries, are very intuitive, so there is a very good chance our models will be well-understood by the audience.

Step 5: Review and confirm

Previously we identified the person or group responsible for validating the model. Now we need to show them the model and make sure it is correct. Often at this stage, after reviewing the model, we make some changes and then show them the model again. This iterative cycle continues until the validator approves the model.

Three tips

1. **Organization**. The steps you went through in building this "model" are the same steps we go through in building any model. It is all about organizing information. Data modelers are fantastic organizers. We take the chaotic real world and show it in a precise form, creating powerful communication tools.

2. **80/20 Rule.** Don't go for perfection. Too many requirements meetings end with unfulfilled goals by spending too much time discussing a minute particular issue. After a few minutes of discussion, if you feel the issue's discussion may take up too much time and not lead to a resolution, document the issue and keep going. You will find that for modeling to work well with Agile and other iterative approaches, you may have to forego perfection and sometimes even completion. Much better to document the unanswered

questions and issues and keep going. Much better to deliver something imperfect yet still very valuable than deliver nothing. You will find that you can get the data model about 80% complete in 20% of the time. One of your deliverables will be a document containing unanswered questions and unresolved issues. Once all of these issues and questions are resolved, which will take about 80% of your time to complete, the model will be 100% complete.

3. **Diplomat.** As William Kent said in **Data and Reality** (1978), *so, once again, if we are going to have a database about books, before we can know what one representative stands for, we had better have a consensus among all users as to what "one book" is.* Invest time trying to get consensus on terms before building a solution. Imagine someone querying on pets without having a clear definition of what a pet is.

Three takeaways

1. Six strategic questions must be asked before you begin any project (Step 1). These questions are a prerequisite to the success of any initiative because they ensure we choose the right terms for our BTM. Next, identify all terms within the scope of the initiative (Step 2). Make sure each term is clearly and completely defined. Then

determine how these terms are related (Step 3). Often, you will need to go back to Step 2 at this point, because in capturing relationships, you may come up with new terms. Next, determine the most beneficial visual for your audience (Step 4). Consider the visual that would resonate best with those needing to review and use your BTM. As a final step, seek approval of your BTM (Step 5). Often at this point, there are additional changes to the model, and we cycle through these steps until the model is accepted.

2. Create a relational BTM in addition to a query BTM if you feel there would be value in capturing and explaining the participation and existence rules.

3. Never underestimate the value of precise and complete definitions.

CHAPTER 2

Refine

This chapter will explain the data modeling refine phase. We explain the purpose of refine, refine the model for our animal shelter case study, and then walk through the refine approach. We end the chapter with three tips and three takeaways.

Purpose

The purpose of the refinement stage is to create the logical data model (LDM) based on our common business vocabulary defined during the align stage. Refine is how the modeler captures the business requirements without complicating the model with implementation concerns, such as software and hardware.

The shelter's Logical Data Model (LDM) uses the common business language from the BTM to precisely define the business requirements. The LDM is fully-attributed yet independent of technology. We build the relational LDM by normalizing, covered in Chapter 1. Figure 48 contains the shelter's relational LDM.

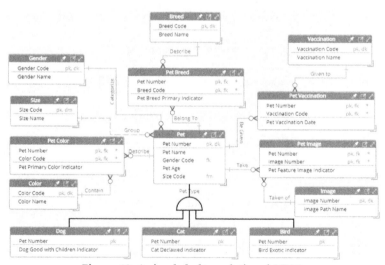

Figure 48: Animal shelter relational LDM.

This model does not change based on requirements. Therefore, we can use it as the starting point model for all queries. Let's briefly walk through the model. The shelter identifies each **Pet** with a **Pet Number**, which is a unique counter assigned to the **Pet** the day the **Pet** arrives. Also entered at this time are the pet's name (**Pet Name**) and age (**Pet Age**). If the **Pet** does not have a name, it is given one by the shelter employee entering the pet's information. If the age is unknown, it is estimated by the shelter employee entering the pet's information. If the **Pet** is a **Dog**, the shelter employee entering the information performs a few assessments to determine whether the Dog is good with children (**Dog Good With Children Indicator**). If the **Pet** is a **Cat**, the shelter employee determines whether the **Cat** has been declawed (**Cat Declawed Indicator**). If the Pet is a **Bird**, the shelter employee enters whether it is an exotic bird such as a parrot (**Bird Exotic Indicator**).

Approach

The refine stage is all about determining the business requirements for the initiative. The end goal is a logical data model which captures the attributes and relationships needed to answer the queries. The steps to complete appear in Figure 49.

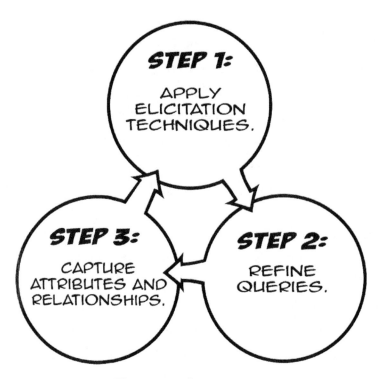

Figure 49: Refinement steps.

Similar to determining the more detailed structures in a traditional logical data model, we determine the more detailed structures needed to deliver the queries during the refinement stage. You can therefore call the query LDM a query refinement model if you prefer. The query refinement model is all about discovery and captures the answers to the queries that reveal insights into a business process.

Step 1: Apply elicitation techniques

This is where we interact with the business stakeholders to identify the attributes and relationships needed to answer the queries. We keep refining, usually until we run out of time. Techniques we can use include interviewing, artifact analysis (studying existing or proposed business or technical documents), job shadowing (watching someone work), and prototyping. You can use any combination of these techniques to obtain the attributes and relationships to answer the queries. Often these techniques are used within an Agile framework. You choose which techniques to use based on your starting point and the needs of the stakeholders. For example, if a stakeholder says, "I don't know what I want, but I'll know when I see it," building a prototype might be the best approach.

Analyze workloads

An important part of this exercise is to identify, quantify, and qualify the workload.

You need to identify each operation as either a read or a write operation, and understand the read-to-write ratio. Make a list of all Create, Read, Update, and Delete (CRUD) operations, and take the time to go through the exercise of drawing wireframes of screens and reports, and of assembling workflow diagrams. Thinking these through and validating them with subject matter experts will inevitably reveal facts you might have previously overlooked.

For write operations, you want to know for how long to hold data, the frequency by which data is transmitted to the system, average document size, retention, and durability. Start your design exercise with the most critical operation and work your way down the list.

For read operations, you also want to document the patterns and required freshness of the data, taking into account eventual consistency and read latency. Data freshness is related to replication time if you read from a secondary, or to the acceptable time for a piece of data derived (computed pattern, for example) from other pieces. It defines how fast written data must be accessible for read operations: immediately (data consistent at all times), within 10 milliseconds, 1 second, 1 minute, 1 hour, or 1 day. For example, reading the top reviews associated with a product, which are cached in the product document, may have a tolerated 1-day freshness. Read latency is specified in milliseconds, where p95 and p99 values represent the 95th and 99th percentile values (a read latency p95 value of 100ms means that 95 out of 100 requests took 100ms or less to complete.)

This information helps validate the choice of design pattern (described later in the book), orients the necessary indexes, and impacts the sizing and provisioning of the hardware, hence the budget for the project. Different data modeling patterns result in different impacts on read performance, number of write operations, cost of indexes, etc. So you may have to make compromises and balance needs that are sometimes contradictory.

You may use a spreadsheet or any other method to document the results of your workload analysis, based on the example in Figure 50, which is built into Hackolade Studio for MongoDB. When considering schema evolution later in the lifecycle, you will be able to review the values originally recorded, as reality might be very different than what was originally estimated. You should document the query predicates with the specific expression and parameters used to determine which documents should be retrieved. A couple of other data points in the form in Figure 50 deserve some clarification.

MongoDB provides different levels of durability options for write operations. These options control how data is written to disk and the level of acknowledgment received from the database:

- **Majority**: a write operation is acknowledged only when it is successfully written to a majority of the replica set members, translating to a write concern of w:majority;
- **One node**: a write operation is acknowledged as soon as it is successfully written to at least one

replica set member, translating to a write concern of w:1;

- **Fire and forget**: MongoDB does not wait for any acknowledgment after the write operation is sent to the server, translating to a write concern of w:0.

Figure 50: Workload analysis data capture screen.

The Search type property allows you to indicate the type of index to define in order to improve the performance of your queries:

- **Standard search**: with this value, we mark queries based on one or more fields in the document, possibly combined in the aggregation pipeline;

- **Geospatial query**: allows for efficient retrieval of documents based on their geographic location or proximity to a specific point for applications with location-based searches or geospatial analysis;

- **Text search**: enables the search for text within text-indexed fields when efficient and relevance-based searches across large volumes of text-based data are required;

- **Lucene search**: this feature of MongoDB Atlas provides a seamless, scalable experience for building applications with complex search capabilities.

The shape of your document and the definition of the index for the collection directly impact the efficiency of your queries. The following values are listed from most efficient to least efficient:

- **Covered query**: the index contains all the queried fields and the necessary data to fulfill the query, eliminating the need for fetching documents from the collection itself;

- **Index seek**: the index quickly locates and retrieves specific documents based on the specified query criteria, minimizing the number of scanned documents;

- **Index scan**: focuses on seeking a specific document or range of documents based on the query predicates, efficiently narrowing down the search;

- **Collection scan**: when no indexes can be used to efficiently filter or locate the desired data, this pattern is resource-intensive and time-consuming, especially for large collections with a significant number of documents.

Quantify relationships

Since the advent of entity relationship diagrams, we restricted ourselves to using zero, one, and many as the different cardinalities of relationships.

This may have been appropriate for the longest time; however, the world has changed. Datasets are a few orders of magnitude larger than they were a few years ago. Not understanding that a relationship's "many" side may refer to thousands or millions of objects and trying to embed, pull, or join these objects may not work well for most applications. Because these humongous relationships are more frequent than before, we suggest quantifying them not just with "many" but with actual numbers. For example, instead of using [0, M] to say that an object can be linked to zero-to-many objects, we should try to quantify these numbers whenever possible. For example, a product may have [0, 1000] reviews. This is more telling. Writing 1000 down makes us think about pagination and possibly limiting the number of reviews on a product when it reaches the maximum value.

To increase our knowledge about the relationship, we can add an optional "most likely" or "median" value. For example, [0, 20, 1000] is more descriptive by telling us that a product may have 0 to 1000 reviews with a median of 20. If we create our model using Hackolade Studio, the arrays in a document can be modeled with the cardinalities in Figure 51.

Quantification ⌄		
Minimum	0	⌃⌄
Min unit	single	⌄
Likely	20	⌃⌄
Likely unit	single	⌄
Maximum	1000	⌃⌄
Max unit	single	⌄

Figure 51: Cardinalities.

And yes, we will get these numbers wrong, especially at the beginning. However, we should get the order of magnitude right. If we don't get it right, it is a red flag to review the model. Maybe a piece of information should not be embedded but referenced instead.

Step 2: Refine queries

The refinement process is iterative, and we keep refining, again, usually until we run out of time.

Step 3: Capture attributes and relationships

Ideally, because of the hierarchical nature of document (and also key-value) databases, we should strive to answer one or more queries with a single structure. Although this might seem "anti-normalization", one structure organized to a particular query is much faster and simpler than connecting multiple structures. The logical data model contains the attributes and related structures needed for each of the queries identified in the query refinement model.

Using artifact analysis, we can start with the animal shelter's logical and use this model as a good way to capture the attributes and relationships within our scope. Based on the queries, quite a few of our concepts are not directly needed for search or filtering, and so they can become additional descriptive attributes on the **Pet** entity.

For example, no critical queries involved vaccinations. Therefore, we can simplify this model subset from the model in Figure 52 to the model in Figure 53.

Figure 52: Normalized model subset.

Figure 53: Denormalized model subset.

This example illustrates how traditional RDBMS models differ from NoSQL. On our original logical model, it was important to communication that a **Pet** can receive many **Vaccinations** and a **Vaccination** can be given to many **Pets**. In NoSQL, however, since there were no queries needing to filter or search by vaccination, the vaccination attributes just become other descriptive attributes of **Pet**.

The **Vaccination Code** and **Vaccination Name** attributes are now a nested array within **Pet**. So, for example, if Spot the Dog had five vaccinations, they would all be listed within Spot's record (or *document* to use MongoDB terminology). Following this same logic, the pet's colors and images also become nested arrays, as shown in Figure 54.

Figure 54: Nested arrays added for color and images.

In addition, to help with querying, we need to create a **Pet Type** structure instead of the subtypes, **Dog**, **Cat**, and **Bird**. After determining the available pets for adoption, we need to distinguish whether the **Pet** is a **Dog**, **Cat**, or **Bird**.

Our model would now look like what appears in Figure 55.

Figure 55: Our complete LDM with Pet Type.

In addition to the denormalization seen before, this example illustrates the polymorphic nature of MongoDB's document model as an alternative to the inheritance tables of relational databases. This single schema describes and can validate different document types for dogs, cats, and birds, in addition to the common structure. Relational subtyping is accomplished here with the oneOf choice which allows multiple subschemas.

Junction tables found in relational models are replaced here by arrays of subobjects, the array data type allowing for an ordered list of items.

Three tips

1. **Access patterns:** the query-driven approach is critical to leverage the benefits of NoSQL when creating an LDM. Don't be tempted by old normalization habits unless the workload analysis reveals relationship cardinality that warrants normalization.

2. **Aggregates:** keep together what belongs together! A nested structure in a single document can ensure atomicity and consistency of inserts, updates, and queries without expensive joins. It is also beneficial for developers who are used to working with objects, and it is easier to understand for humans.

3. **It is easier to normalize a denormalized structure than the opposite:** a normalized LDM is not technology-agnostic if it includes supertypes/subtypes

or junction tables. Or it is "technology-agnostic" only if your physical targets are exclusively relational and don't include NoSQL. A denormalized LDM on the other hand, can be easily normalized for relational physical targets by a good data modeling tool, while providing denormalized structures based on the access patterns identified earlier.

Three takeaways

1. The purpose of the refinement stage is to create the logical data model (LDM) based on our common business vocabulary, defined for our initiative during the align stage. Refine is how the modeler captures the business requirements without complicating the model with implementation concerns, such as software and hardware.

2. An LDM is typically fully-attributed yet independent of technology. But this strict definition is being challenged nowadays with the fact that technology targets can be so different in nature: relational databases, the different families of NoSQL, storage formats for data lakes, pub/sub pipelines, APIs, etc.

3. It used to be, with relational databases, that you wanted to design a structure that could handle any possible future query that might be run down the road.

With NoSQL, you want to design schemas that are specific, not only for an application, but for each access pattern (write or read) in that application.

CHAPTER 3

Design

This chapter will explain the data modeling design phase. We explain the purpose of design, design the model for our animal shelter case study, and then walk through the design approach. We end the chapter with three tips and three takeaways.

Purpose

The purpose of the design stage is to create the physical data model (PDM) based on the business requirements defined on our logical data model. Design is how the modeler captures the technical requirements without compromising the business requirements, yet accommodating the initiative's software and technology needs used for the initiative.

The design stage is also where we accommodate history. That is, we modify our structures to capture how data changes over time. For example, the Design stage would allow us to keep track of not just the most recent name for a pet, but also the original. For example, the animal shelter changes a pet's name from Sparky to Daisy. Our design could store the original pet name and the most current, so we would know Daisy's original name was Sparky. Although this is not a book on temporal data or modeling approaches that gracefully allow for storing high data volatility or varying history requirements, such as the Data Vault,[4] you would need to consider such factors in the Design stage.

Figure 56 shows the Physical Data Model (PDM) of the animal shelter's Microsoft Access database design.

---

[4] For more on the data vault, read John Giles' *The Elephant in the Fridge*.

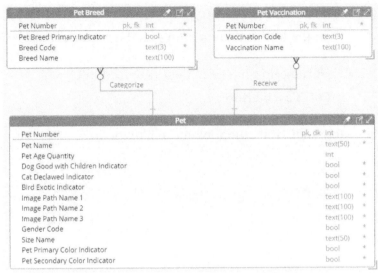

Figure 56: PDM of the shelter's Access database.

Note that the PDM includes formatting and nullability. Also, this model is heavily denormalized. For example:

- Although the logical communicates that a **Pet** can have any number of images, their design only allows up to three images for each **Pet**. The shelter uses **Image_Path_Name_1** for the featured image.

- Notice how the decode entities from the logical have been addressed. The one-to-many relationships are denormalized into **Pet**. **Gender_Name** is not needed because everyone knows the codes. People are not familiar with **Size_Code** so only **Size_Name** is stored. **Breed** has been denormalized into **Pet_Breed**. It is common for decode entities to be modeled in different ways on the physical, depending on the requirements.

- **Vaccination** has been denormalized into **Pet_Vaccination**.

For MongoDB, it would look more like the model in Figure 57.

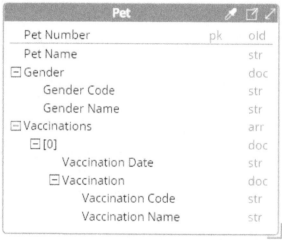

Figure 57: If modeling the shelter's Access database in MongoDB.

Approach

The design stage is all about developing the database-specific design for the initiative. The end goal is the query PDM, which we can also call the *query design model*. For our animal shelter initiative, this model captures the MongoDB design and JSON interchange format for the initiative. The steps to complete appear in Figure 58.

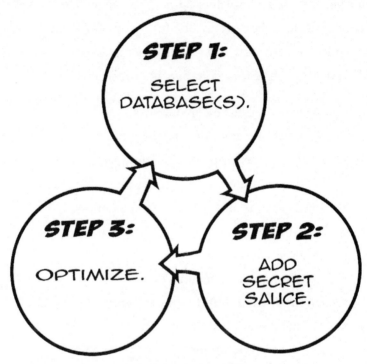

Figure 58: Design steps.

Step 1: Select database(s)

We now know enough to decide which database would be ideal for the application. Sometimes we might choose more than one database if we feel it would be the best architecture for the application. We know in the consortium's case that they are using JSON for transport and MongoDB for storage.

Step 2: Add secret sauce

Although document NoSQL databases can be quite similar, each database has something special to consider during design. For example, for MongoDB, we would consider where to use their secret sauce, such as MongoDB-specific functionality like the following:

- Indexes (multi-key, geo, search, …)
- Replication for shorter latency
- Sharding for supporting humongous databases
- MongoDB Query and Aggregation Languages
- Explicit joins and recursive joins between documents
- Schema validation
- Read and write concerns
- Change streams and Atlas triggers
- Transactions
- Document Archiving
- Time-series collections
- Lucene-based search
- Security features, from basic authentication to Field Level Encryption to satisfy complex requirements like the right to be forgotten in GDPR.

Embedding vs. referencing

Embedding

When you model for MongoDB, embedding is commonly seen for any type of relationship. Choosing whether to embed or reference a relationship will lead to a different solution in each case. Making the right decision for each relationship will give you the best model among all possible models.

In a relational database model, one-to-one relationships tend to be embedded. The two pieces of information live in the same row. In the case of one-to-many or many-to-many relationships, the two pieces of information are divided into different rows in different tables. With MongoDB, embedding a one-to-one relationship means putting the two pieces of information in the same document. You could also opt to use a subdocument to group related information, such as the components of an address:

```
// A one-to-one relationship within a subdocument
{
    "_id": "dog19370824",
    "name": "Champ",
    "address": {
        "street": "1600 Pennsylvania Avenue NW",
        "city": "Washington",
        "state": "DC",
        "zip": "20500",
        "country": "USA",
    }
}
```

You embed a one-to-many relationship with an array or a dictionary. An array is the document construct to express a one-to-many relationship in the document model.

```
// a Pet document with embedded Pet comments
{
  "_id": "dog19370824",
  "name": "Fanny",
  "comments": [ {
     "name": "Daniel Coupal",
     "text": "Fanny is the sweetest dog ever!"
   }, {
     "name": "Steve Hoberman",
     "text": "Fanny loved my daughter's brownies."
   } ]
}
```

For a many-to-many relationship, we also use an array or a dictionary. It is important to note that embedding this type of relationship may introduce data duplication. Data duplication is not necessarily bad for your model; however, we want to highlight the difference with embedding a one-to-many relationship where it does not introduce denormalization or data duplication in contrast with the many-to-many relationship.

Referencing

We reference another document by using a scalar if the relationship is a "one" or with an array of "references" if the relationship is a "many." References can be unidirectional or bi-directional. Using the example of Pets and related comments, we can describe the relationship as:

"A Pet may have many comments" and "A comment must be associated with a Pet," getting different alternatives to express the references as illustrated in the examples that follow. Example of references from the parent's document:

```
// References from the parent document to the child
documents using an array
//
// a Pet document with references to Comment
documents
{
    "_id": "dog19370824",
    "name": "Fanny",
    "comments": [
        "comment101",
        "comment102"
    ]
}
// referenced Comment documents
{
    "_id": "comment01",
    "name": "Daniel Coupal",
    "text": "Fanny is the sweetest dog ever!"
},
{
    "_id": "comment102",
    "name": "Steve Hoberman",
    "text": "Fanny loved my daughter's brownies."
}
```

Examples of references from the children's documents:

```
// References from a child document to the parent
document
//
// a Pet document
{
```

```
    "_id": "dog19370824",
    "name": "Fanny
}
// Comment documents with reference to the parent
document
{
    "_id": "comment01",
    "dog": "dog19370824",
    "name": "Daniel Coupal",
    "text": "Fanny is the sweetest dog ever!"
},
{
    "_id": "comment102",
    "dog": "dog19370824",
    "name": "Steve Hoberman",
    "text": "Fanny loved my daughter's brownies."
}
```

Example of bi-directional references:

```
// References from the parent document to the child
documents and vice-versa
//
// a Pet document with references to Comment
documents
{
    "_id": "dog19370824",
    "name": "Fanny",
    "comments": [
        "comment101",
        "comment102"
    ]
}

// referenced Comment documents with reference to the
parent document
{
    "_id": "comment01",
    "dog": "dog19370824",
    "name": "Daniel Coupal",
```

```
    "text": "Fanny is the sweetest dog ever!"
},
{
    "_id": "comment102",
    "dog": "dog19370824",
    "name": "Steve Hoberman",
    "text": "Fanny loved my daughter's brownies."
}
```

Note that a relational model would usually not have an array of "pets." Joins in relational databases support scalar values, so references are not implemented in both directions. With MongoDB, only use the references on the side from which you want to access the other objects. Maintaining bidirectional references is more expensive to manage. To summarize referencing, use a scalar to reference a "one" and an array to reference a "many." Add the references in the main objects from which you will query the data.

Rules and guidelines to choose between embedding and referencing

To decide which model to use between embedding and referencing, the main rules are "what is used together in the application is stored together in the database" and "prefer embedding over referencing." Let's explain these two main rules.

Keep everything that is used together in the application together in the database to avoid doing many joins or reads. Joins are costly in terms of CPU and I/O access.

Avoiding joins gives much better performance. If each occurrence of the essential query goes from doing three reads and two joins to only one read where the three pieces are embedded, you may have just slashed your hardware requirements by a factor of three.

As you keep what you need together, you may want to avoid bloating the document by excluding unnecessary information. The reason is that reading this document will take up more space in memory, limiting the number of documents you can keep in memory at a given time.

Our second main rule asks that we prefer embedding to referencing. The main reason is that complete objects are usually more straightforward for your application, simpler to archive, and do not require transactions to be updated atomically. In other words, you choose simplicity over complexity by embedding over referencing.

With these two rules in mind, let's look at additional guidelines to help us decide between embedding or referencing. To illustrate the guidelines, we will use an example of a financial application where we have a relationship between people and credit cards. The application is developed by a bank subject to all kinds of financial regulations. Based on the questions we saw earlier in the book, we establish that this is a one-to-many relationship that reads, "a person may have many credit cards" and "a card must be owned by a person." And because our system is making requests about people more than cards, the primary entity of that relationship is the person, not the card. Table 6 below lists the additional guidelines.

The first guideline is "Simplicity." This is directly related to our rule in favor of embedding. The related question is: Would keeping the pieces of information together lead to a simpler data model and code? In our example, having one object in the code for a person with their credit cards gives us a simpler code.

The second guideline is "Go Together." The related question is: Do the pieces of information have a "has-a," "contains," or similar relationship? Here we try to understand the dependence of one piece of information on the other. A person "has-a" credit card, so let's answer 'yes.'

The third guideline is "Query Atomicity." The related question is: Does the application query the pieces of information together? Again, we usually want to load the person's info with the credit cards together in the application, so let's again answer 'yes.'

The fourth guideline is "Update Complexity." The related question is: Are the pieces of information updated together? Not really. We will probably add credit cards without modifying the person's information.

Guideline Name	Question	Embed	Reference
Simplicity	Would keeping the pieces of information together lead to a simpler data model and code?	Yes	
Go Together	Do the pieces of information have a "has-a," "contains," or similar relationship?	Yes	
Query Atomicity	Does the application query the pieces of information together?	Yes	
Update Complexity	Are the pieces of information updated together?	Yes	
Archival	Should the pieces of information be archived at the same time?	Yes	
Cardinality	Is there a high cardinality (current or growing) in a "many" side of the relationship?	No	Yes
Data Duplication	Would data duplication be too complicated to manage and undesired?	No	Yes
Document Size	Would the combined size of the pieces of information take too much memory or transfer bandwidth for the application?	No	Yes
Document Growth	Would the embedded piece grow without bound?	No	Yes
Workload	Are the pieces of information written at different times in a write-heavy workload?		Yes
Individuality	For the children's side of the relationship, can the pieces exist by themselves without a parent?		Yes

Table 6: Embed versus reference guidelines.

Let's pause here. We answered 'yes' three times, leading to choosing 'embedding.' But what happened when we answered 'no'? For the first four rules, a 'no' has no impact. In other words, answering 'no' does not favor 'embedding,' but it also does not tell us we should 'reference.'

The fifth guideline is "Archival." The related question is: Should the pieces of information be archived at the same time? As in our example, this question is only relevant if the system must archive data for regulatory reasons. This guideline is related to the archive schema design pattern we describe later in the book. The essence is that it is easier to archive a single document with all the information in it than a bunch of smaller pieces that would need to be reattached or joined together in the future when looking at the archived information. It is a 'yes.' When a user account is deactivated, we want the card information at that time to also be archived.

The sixth guideline is "Cardinality." The related question is: Is there a high cardinality (current or growing) in the "many" side of the relationship? No person should have a few hundred or a thousand cards. This guideline does not just favor "referencing" in the affirmative. It favors "embedding" in the negative. This reflects the bias we have toward preferring "embedding." If the answer is 'yes,' we want to avoid embedding large arrays. These large arrays make for large documents, and by experience, we know that usually, the information in large arrays is not entirely needed all the time with the base document.

The seventh guideline is "Data Duplication." The related question is: Would data duplication be too complicated to manage and undesired? A one-to-many relationship does not generate data duplication, so we have a 'no' to this question.

The eighth guideline is "Document Size." The related question is: Would the combined size of the pieces of information take too much memory or transfer bandwidth for the application? This is related to the large arrays question, as most big documents contain such large arrays. But here, we want to go further. The document must only be considered 'big' by the consuming application. If it is a mobile application, we are likely more conscious about how much data is transferred. For our example, the total size should be relatively small, even for our mobile applications.

The ninth guideline is "Document Growth." The related question is: Would the embedded piece grow without bound? This question is also related to the document size. However, it also factors in the impact of often updating the same document by adding new elements in arrays. Keeping the information in different documents will make for smaller write operations. In our example, the documents would have little growth over time.

The tenth guideline is "Workload." The related question is: Are the pieces of information written at different times in a write-heavy workload? A write-heavy workload will benefit from writing to different documents and avoiding the contention of writing to the same documents often. The example would be a write-heavy workload only if we produce thousands of cards every second.

The eleventh guideline is "Individuality." The related question is: For the children's side of the relationship, can the pieces exist by themselves without a parent? For our example, let's say 'no.' A card must have an owner printed on it before we add it to the system. If the card could exist without an owner, then embedding the card into a person would cause an issue when we delete the owner, and the card must continue to exist. Relationships, where both sides may exist alone, are better modeled with separate documents.

Tallying the results, it is clear that we should embed the credit cards with the person. If we had answers for both "embedding" and "referencing," we would consider the priority of each guideline regarding our application requirements.

In the case of ambiguity between "embedding" and "referencing," it would make this relationship a good candidate to apply a schema design pattern, which we will discuss later.

Guideline Name	Question	Embed	Reference
Simplicity	Would keeping the pieces of information together lead to a simpler data model and code?	Yes	
Go Together	Do the pieces of information have a "has-a," "contains," or similar relationship?	Yes	
Query Atomicity	Does the application query the pieces of information together?	Yes	
Update Complexity	Are the pieces of information updated together?	Yes	
Archival	Should the pieces of information be archived at the same time?	Yes	
Cardinality	Is there a high cardinality (current or growing) in a "many" side of the relationship?	No	Yes
Data Duplication	Would data duplication be too complicated to manage and undesired?	No	Yes
Document Size	Would the combined size of the pieces of information take too much memory or transfer bandwidth for the application?	No	Yes
Document Growth	Would the embedded piece grow without bound?	No	Yes
Workload	Are the pieces of information written at different times in a write-heavy workload?		Yes
Individuality	For the children's side of the relationship, can the pieces exist by themselves without a parent?		Yes

Table 7: Example of choosing between embedding and referencing.

Schema design patterns

Our role with this book is to make you aware of all of the possibilities, cover the pros and cons, and share use cases. This should inspire readers as they design their schemas. It is a toolbox. Then it is up to the reader to choose the most appropriate tool for their use cases.

MongoDB design patterns are reusable solutions for many of the commonly occurring use cases encountered when designing applications that leverage persistence in MongoDB.

Note that you don't necessarily need to use the same pattern for reads and for writes. CQRS (which stands for "Command and Query Responsibility Segregation") is an architecture pattern that prescribes splitting the query operations from the write/update operations. This separation of concerns can bring more flexibility, improved scalability, and enhanced performance. The higher complexity, however, implies a steeper learning curve and higher development costs. With eventual consistency, there's also a challenge to ensure that data synchronization is performed in the application, via pub/sub pipelines, or with the transactional capabilities available since MongoDB 4.0.

It is not because a pattern exists that you should use it. Using the wrong pattern for a particular use case can be damaging. For example, don't automatically normalize because that's what you're used to doing with relational databases. Involve subject matter experts to ensure that the design satisfies the business needs, not just the developers' convenience. Take into consideration the access patterns. Optimize the user experience. Leverage workflow diagrams, CRUD wireframes, and documented workload analysis. Use an Entity-Relationship Diagram for your PDM to engage in a dialog with all the application stakeholders. Iterate enough times to think through the details. Validate schema designs. Realize that the schema will evolve over time as new requirements appear or as reality sheds a new light on assumptions.

There are a few ways to think about *Schema Design Patterns* (SDP) considering their categorization, difficulty of usage, and application.

The *Computation* category contains patterns that pre-calculate or assemble data to speed up operations.

The *Grouping* category contains patterns that combine many or parts of documents into a single document.

The *Lifecycle* category contains patterns that have *Operations*. Operations are scripts or procedures that are performed outside of the application at a given time in the system's lifecycle.

The *Polymorphism* category contains patterns designed around the polymorphic characteristic of the document model. If you need a refresher on polymorphism, please refer to the "About the Book" section on page 14. This characteristic allows objects with different shapes to live in one collection for various reasons.

The *Relationships* category contains patterns that go beyond simply embedding or referencing to model the relationships between documents. For example, patterns in this category may pivot data or model graphs.

Table 8 summarizes our *Schema Design Patterns* grouped by categories.

Category	Patterns
Computation	• Approximation • Computed
Grouping	• Bucket • Outlier • Preallocated
Lifecycle	• Archive • Document Versioning • Envelope • Schema Versioning
Polymorphism	• Inheritance • Single Collection
Relationships	• Attribute • Extended Reference • Graph • Subset • Tree

Table 8: Schema design patterns by category.

We also group patterns based on how easy they are to understand and how frequently we encounter them.

The list below of the basic six patterns is an excellent place to start, as they are the easiest to understand. The following five are quite advanced patterns, meaning they are more difficult to understand or implement; however, they may bring a lot of performance improvements to the application. Finally, for completeness, we have five more patterns that we use less frequently. Nevertheless, they have their place in some designs. Table 9 summarizes *Schema Design Patterns* by their difficulty level.

Difficulty	Patterns
Basic	• Approximation • Computed • Extended Reference • Inheritance • Envelope • Schema Versioning
Advanced	• Archive • Attribute • Bucket • Single Collection • Subset
Less common	• Document Versioning • Graph Pattern • Outlier • Preallocated • Tree

Table 9: Schema design patterns by difficulty.

Table 10 illustrates some attributes of each pattern. One important attribute is the introduction or not of anomalies. If you recall, anomalies refer to data duplication, staleness, and broken referential integrity.

Pattern	Category	Model Relationship (Yes/No)	Introduce Anomalies (S=some)
Approximation	Computation	N	Y
Archive	Lifecycle	N	N
Attribute	Relationship	Y	N
Bucket	Grouping	Y	N
Computed	Computation	N	Y
Document Versioning	Lifecycle	N	N
Envelope	Lifecycle	N	N
Extended Reference	Relationship	Y	Y
Graph	Relationship	Y	S
Inheritance	Polymorphism	Y	N
Outlier	Grouping	Y	N
Preallocated	Grouping	Y	N
Schema Versioning	Lifecycle	N	N
Single Collection	Polymorphism	Y	N
Subset	Relationship	Y	Y
Tree	Relationship	Y	S

Table 10: Some attributes of schema design patterns.

Finally, we illustrate each pattern with scenarios that use it. Selecting five domains (Financial Services, E-commerce,

Internet of Things, Customer Service, and a Web Site) and a typical application for each domain, we illustrate a specific requirement that may benefit from applying a given pattern.

Our Advisor application for the Financial Services domain allows different advisors to manage their direct clients. The advisors use the application to get a complete picture of clients and track their interactions. In other words, it is like a Customer Relationship Management system for the advisors.

The Shopping site for the e-commerce domain is similar to Amazon, Walmart, and other sites where we shop.

The SIM Cards system for the Internet of Things (IoT) domain is a solution to connect many devices (cars, fridges, etc.) to a single monitoring system. In this case, the devices use the cellular network to communicate with the server using SIM cards.

The Single View application for the Customer Service domain is an application to provide a complete view of a customer in a complex environment. For example, an insurance company may have acquired many competitors over the years. Merging all the legacy databases into one single MongoDB database is a very common scenario. The single database allows a customer support representative to see all the information regarding one customer easily and quickly.

And finally, the Movies site is a typical web site with reference data. The site has many concurrent users; therefore, we prepare the data to be quickly accessed and displayed in a browser or mobile application.

We will need to be very creative to make use of every pattern in the context of the Pet Adoption application. Some of the new requirements may look funny; hopefully, you will think they are. Play with your imagination with the following additional requirements.

- Track, if available, the pet's mother.

- Let people comment on breeds to help other users decide if this is the right breed for them.

- Record the pet room for each pet.

- Allow a pet to have a Twitter account. Some are real celebrities with a lot of followers. These pets are too valuable; they are not up for adoption.

- Allow visitors to interact with our pets. We are required to keep a record of the interactions.

- Keep these visitor interactions for the duration of the pet's stay, or in the case of our permanent residents, the pet's life.

- Enable users to purchase pet celebrity swag and merchandise through our online store.

Pattern	Financial Services (Advisor app)	E-commerce (Shopping site)	IoT (SIM cards)	Customer Service (Single View)	Website (Movies site)
Approximation		Web page counters	Counter for connected devices		Web page counters
Archive	Keep documents for audits	Discontinued products	Keep measurements for analytics		
Attribute	Search for customers' info	Product attributes		Document searchable criterias	Movie revenues per selected countries
Bucket	Transaction per account per month		Measurements for a day	Claims per account per year	Movie revenues per day
Computed	Value of accounts at end of day		Sums and averages per bucket		Revenues from ticket sales
Document Versioning	Audit trail on changes	Changes in the last month			
Envelope	Application migration, lineage	Application migration, lineage	Application migration, lineage	Application migration, lineage	Application migration, lineage
Extended Reference	Accounts in customer profile	Products in order	Device in measurement	Customer in policy	Actor in movie
Graph	Investigating fraudulent transactions between individuals	Multi-categories product hierarchy			
Inheritance	Grouping different credit products	Grouping different product types	Grouping SIMs from different manufacturers	Grouping policies	Grouping movies and TV shows
Outlier					List of extras
Pre-allocated	Scheduling meetings with advisors		Measurements for a day		Seats in a theater
Schema Versioning	Application updates	Application updates	Application updates	Application updates	Application updates
Single Collection		Shopping cart		User profiles, policies, claims, and messages	
Subset	Last transactions in an account	Product's reviews	Recently reported data for a device	Log of customer's interactions	Movie's reviews
Tree	Bank locations organization	Product categories	Regions organization where devices are located		Assembling policies with fragments

Table 11: Schema design patterns, use cases, and scenarios.

The Approximation Pattern

What is the population of the Earth? Because people are born and die every second, the number changes constantly. Any number we say is wrong the moment we say it. Even numbers reported by national organizations are off, as it is a collection of different measures done at other times.

Should we obsess about finding the exact number? No, first because it is challenging to calculate, and second because our numbers are good enough. Often, we fall into the trap of trying to get the perfect number when an approximation is good enough.

Although perfect numbers are great, the cost to get them may be more than it is worth.

Overall description of the Approximation Pattern

The *Approximation Pattern*'s goal is to save resources. In today's large systems, a simple operation can magnify to a point where the result is not worth the cost of the effort. The *Approximation Pattern* will replace this too-costly operation with something good enough and more cost-effective.

The *Approximation Pattern* works well for tracking web page counters. It is a good choice for keeping track of numbers that grow consistently.

If approximations are unacceptable due to the imprecisions they introduce, consider using the *Computed Pattern*.

The *Approximation Pattern* has the following variants:

- Buffering the writes.
- Applying constant random writes.
- Applying geometrical random writes.

Details of the Approximation Pattern

Let's use the e-commerce use case. One of the requirements of our system is to count the number of times customers view our products. This counter tracks the number of views in the product document. This counter helps us calculate a ratio between the views and sales. The ratio identifies which pages incite the customers to buy our products.

Now, let's assume a trendy smartphone gets released and that 10 million people see the page for this new product in the first hour of the release. If we increment a counter for the page views, we record 10 million writes over one hour, the equivalent of 3000 writes per second just for this one product. This high number of writes probably outnumbers all the other writes to record the sales across all products. In other words, this counter could consume up to 80% (we made up this number) of the cluster's resources. In this scenario, the system wields most of the resources to keep track of the page views instead of focusing on the business core.

If having the exact number of page views is crucial, let's pay for the infrastructure to keep the precise counts. However, do we need this precision? Is the last number significant? Or are the last two digits significant? If the last two digits are deemed insignificant, we could increment the counter by 100, 1/100 of the time. On large numbers, the precision lost is negligible.

The design increments the value by X for 1/X of the observations.

```
if random(0..99) == 0:
    increment = 100
else:
    increment = 0
```

Returning to our example, we now write 100,000 times per hour, the equivalent of 30 writes per second, instead of the original 10,000,000 times per hour. We can apply a more considerable interval value if there are still too many writes.

The larger the interval we increment, the larger the introduced error. And the impact is more significant on a small counter. A page viewed 70 times would show a counter value of 100 or 0 for an interval of 100, a best case of an error of 30%. A page viewed 7000 times is more likely to be off by only a few hundred, giving an error rate of less than 10%. We should expect an error rate of 1% or less as the counter grows.

The above design is a simple algorithm. There are a lot of alternate algorithms in the literature. A slightly more complex algorithm may use a different interval based on the current value of the counter. For example, we only approximate a counter value of 100 or greater. The counter is incremented every time by 1. For counters values between 100 and 10000, we use an approximation of 10. For numbers between 10000 and 1,000,000, we use an approximation of 100, and so on.

Reducing the number of writes also helps the system with concurrency. If the counter resides in one document per product, this document will undergo massive concurrent locks and potential write conflicts.

The counter is a good example of using the *Approximation Pattern*. We have seen it often in production at customer sites.

There are a few other situations where the *Approximation Pattern* would apply. Usually, the cases fall into one of the following categories.

- Data is difficult to calculate correctly.
- Data is expensive to calculate.
- Imprecise numbers are acceptable.

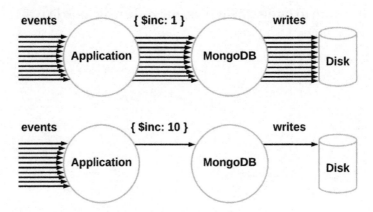

Figure 59: Writes to disk.

Implementing the Approximation Pattern

To implement the *Approximation Pattern*, take the following steps.

Modify the application's business logic to handle the frequency of the writes and the payload of these writes. The *Approximation Pattern* does not require any changes in the schema.

As described earlier, the following snippet would introduce an approximation and divide by 100 the number of writes for a given value.

```
if random(0..99) == 0:
    increment = 100
    db.collection.write({mycounter: increment})
else:
    // do nothing
    increment = 0
```

If we are to buffer the writes, the code may look like the following.

```
counter = counter + 1
if counter == 100:
    db.collection.write({mycounter: counter})
    counter = 0
else:
    // do nothing
...
on_termination(counter):
    db.collection.write({mycounter: counter})
```

Example of applying the Approximation Pattern with the pet adoption use case

Counters are a common requirement in most systems, so it is with our Pet Adoption project. Let's use the *Approximation Pattern* to model web page counters for our site.

As discussed in the implementation section, this pattern is easy to implement on the Data Modeling side; add the counter to the appropriate document.

In this case, we will add a web_page_views to the pet document. An example of a document looks like this.

```
// a Pet document with a counter for the web page
views.
{
    "_id": "bird102345",
    "pet_name": "Lady G",
    ...
    "web_page_views": "1934127"
}
```

The schema for this document is super simple and looks like the model in Figure 60.

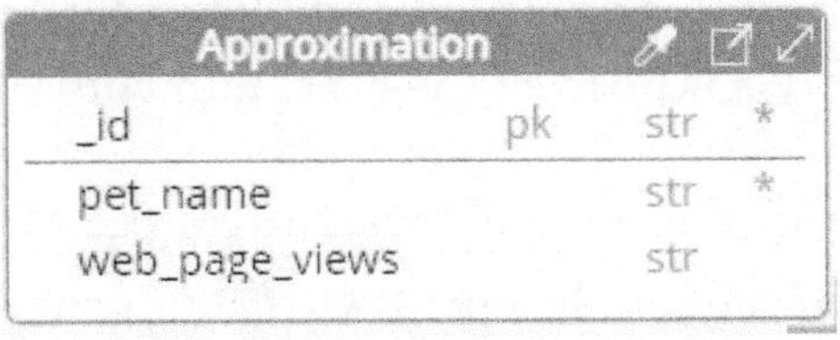

Approximation			
_id	pk	str	*
pet_name		str	*
web_page_views		str	

Figure 60: Approximation schema example.

Finally, we add the function that will update the counters in the code.

Benefits of the Approximation Pattern

When write operations bind the system, applying this pattern can easily divide the share of writes by the counters by 10, 100, or 1000. In other words, the percentage of writes for the counters goes from the prominent share to negligible.

If we model the counter as one field in one document, having many threads trying to increment the counter simultaneously will likely generate some write conflicts. This type of conflict is handled gracefully by MongoDB's storage engine with a retry. However, these retries are wasting resources and queueing the processes. It is preferable to avoid them.

The pattern produces a value, which any approximation could do. This value is a statistically valid number.

Trade-offs with the Approximation Pattern

The *Approximation Pattern* introduces an "anomaly" for the fields the pattern targets. The anomaly produces results that may vary a little from the exact numbers.

In the case of the variant that buffers the writes, it will remain accurate if all processes can flush their writes before exiting. Any deviation will lead to some offsets over time. The reported numbers will always be exact or lower than the expected numbers.

Another trade-off is the added complexity in the code. Instead of doing a simple write operation that increments a counter, the application will need to generate a random number and check if this number triggers a write.

Summary of the Approximation Pattern

The *Approximation Pattern* is a simple pattern that helps reduce resource usage for data that can be imperfect. One implements this pattern within the application.

Problem	• High resource usage from write operations for keeping a perfect state where it is not required.
Solution	• Reduce the frequency of write operations. • Increase the payload done by the write operations.

Use cases	• Web page counters.
	• Other high-value counters.
	• Statistics.
Benefits	• Reduces the number of write operations.
	• Reduces write operation contention on documents.
	• Statistically valid numbers.
Trade-offs	• Potentially creates imperfect numbers.
	• Must be implemented in the application.

Table 12: The Approximation Pattern.

The Archive Pattern

What if the project demands that the data be kept around forever? If so, someone is a data hoarder.

On a more serious note, a project may need to keep data indefinitely due to regulatory requirements or other valid reasons. Paying good money to keep data over, let's say, seven years when the queries only use the data from the last three months is not a good strategy.

Overall description of the Archive Pattern

The *Archive Pattern* answers a familiar customer request about tiering data. In other words, a way to store less frequently used data in cheaper storage. Here is a typical example of such requirements:

1. Store data less than two years old in the database.

2. Store data aged between two to seven years in cheaper file storage. Some common choices are S3, glacier, or a less expensive cluster.

3. Delete data that is older than seven years.

We frequently see the *Archives Pattern* in applications governed by banking, pharmaceutical, or other regulations. We use the pattern to put aside obsolete objects, such as products no longer in demand. We do so when those comprise a significant percentage of the total number of objects. Another common scenario is archiving old logs and IoT measurements.

If it is necessary to keep all document versions, not just the latest, refer to the *Document Versioning Pattern*.

The *Archive Pattern* has these variants:

- Archiving to file storage.
- Archiving to a less expensive cluster.
- Archiving to another collection in the same cluster.

Details of the Archive Pattern

To utilize this pattern, we need two locations. The first location is for the frequently accessed documents, such as those less than two years old. Usually, the core database storage will hold these documents.

We want the second location to be less expensive than the first location. Here are three common choices for the second location:

- External file storage.
- A collection in a less expensive cluster.
- A separate collection in the same database.

File storage (like Amazon's S3) is much cheaper for storing documents. On the other hand, the cost to query the data is much higher. File storage solutions like this make reading a single document hard without reading a large file section. Nevertheless, it is the most popular choice for archiving.

The second alternative copies the document to another less expensive cluster. We pick a smaller-scale cluster because the workload has fewer operations, and it is acceptable to have a long latency for queries. In this solution, there is little saving on storage but more on computing resources like CPU and RAM. Contrary to external file storage, queries are less expensive in this solution. It is still a MongoDB collection providing direct access to documents and using indexes.

The third alternative also copies the documents to another collection in the same cluster. There is no saving on storage. The documents take up the same amount of space; however, there is less need to index the old documents. Savings occur by preventing older documents from taking space in the precious RAM of the server.[5] Similar to the previous solution, older documents are no longer in the working set. When the application needs to access older documents, the query should use a secondary replica or an analytics node.

---

[5] Collection scans have a less negative impact if the old documents are not in the same collection anymore.

Implementing the Archive Pattern

To implement the *Archive Pattern*, take the following steps:

- Favor embedding relationships. The ideal document selected for archiving contains all its relationships. When it is time to answer an audit, we want to avoid reconstructing a document from many pieces for it to make sense.

- Have one field in the document containing the age of the document.

- Set the document age field to "Keep forever" for documents that should never expire or should not move to the archive.

- Elect an alternative location to store the archived documents.

- Create a script or modify the application to archive or delete documents.

- Determine a schedule for archiving and deleting documents.[6]

MongoDB Atlas' archival feature handles steps 4., 5., and 6. seamlessly.

_____

[6] A TTL index could help with deleting documents.

Example of applying the Archive Pattern with the pet adoption use case

One of the Pet Adoption project's requirements is to archive all the interactions of our pets. We use the *Archive Pattern* to archive our pets' interactions. We are archiving the interactions our pets have for the length of their stay with us or, in the case of our celebrity pets, keeping the interactions until our celebrities "cross the rainbow." Once the interactions are three months old, we will move them to an archive. If these older documents were going to be read once in a while, we should keep them in another collection, either in the same cluster or another cluster. In this case, the same cluster seems more appropriate.

We suspect older interactions rarely need to be read, so let's move them to the third storage tier. Our choice for this cheaper tier is S3 files. Most similar file base storage that implements the AWS S3 functionality will do. First, let's look at the documents that we want to archive. The documents must have two characteristics: a date for the archiving and enough information so the documents make sense when we retrieve them. In other words, any reference to another document still needs to exist.

```
// an Interaction document with a bucket of
// monthly interactions
{
    "_id": {
        "pet_id": "bird102345",
        "month": ISODate("2023-02-01T00:00:00Z")
    },
```

```
    "interactions": [
        {
            "ts": ISODate("2023-02-14T22:14:00Z"),
            "userid": 34717
        },
        {
            "ts": ISODate("2023-02-15T20:00:00Z"),
            "userid": 31043
        }
    ]
}
```

Figure 61 shows the schema for the above document.

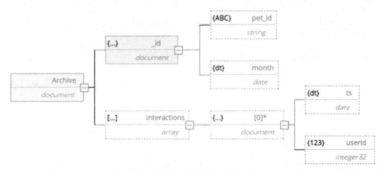

Figure 61: Archive schema example.

Figure 62 shows the schema tree view.

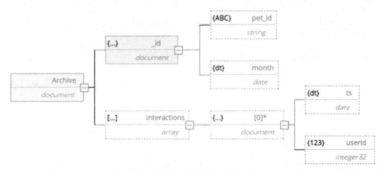

Figure 62: Schema tree view.

The field $month is what we need to archive, so we are good. As for the references to other documents, we have

the userid field. We should be good if these userid
values are available over the pet's life. Still, it makes
reading and searching through documents a complex
operation. So, let's apply the *Extended Reference Pattern* and
add the name corresponding to the userid field. The same
applies to the _id, a reference to our Pet document. We
will also use the Extended Reference Pattern to bring our
pet's name. Now, the document looks like the following.

```
// an Interaction document with a bucket of monthly
// interactions with extended references
{
    "_id": {
        "pet_id": "bird102345",
        "month": ISODate("2023-02-01T00:00:00Z")
    },
    "pet_name": "Lady G", // Extended Reference
    "month": ISODate("2023-02-01T00:00:00Z"),
    "interactions": [
        {
            "ts": ISODate("2023-02-14T22:14:00Z"),
            "userid": 34717,
            "name": "Daniel Coupal" // Ext Ref
        },
        {
            "ts": ISODate("2023-02-15T20:00:00Z"),
            "userid": 31043,
            "name": "Pascal Desmarets" // Ext Ref
        }
    ]
}
```

Figure 63 shows the schema for the above document.

Figure 63: Extended reference pattern schema example.

Now, we need a query to find all documents older than three months. A script will run the query periodically, once a month should do, then copy the documents in the S3 location and complete by deleting the documents in our database.

```
db.interactions.aggregate([
  {
    $match:
      {
        month: {
          $lt: new Date(
            new Date().setMonth(
              new Date().getMonth() - 3
            )
          ),
        },
      },
  },
])
```

Benefits of the Archive Pattern

One of the main goals of the *Archive Pattern* is to reduce the costs of managing older documents. If the costs are already low, applying this pattern is unnecessary.

The other main goal is to satisfy the regulatory requirements to keep data for an extended time. If preserving the documents in the main database for many years is not deemed too expensive, applying the pattern is unnecessary.

Trade-offs with the Archive Pattern

Because archived documents live on slower data storage, possibly not indexes, retrieving these documents is slower. Sometimes the cost per retrieval is higher because there are no indexes, like in the case of S3 files. So we must ensure that the archival does not translate to higher costs.

We can query across many sources using the federation mode using the MongoDB Atlas' archive functionality. In this case, a single query will request the data from the database and the archive. This federated query may not exist in our environment, which is fine if we don't need it. When we need it, an API service assembling the data from many sources should satisfy the requirements.

Updating data that is archived is often a challenge. In-place updates are often not supported by lower tiers like

S3. If this is a crucial requirement, alternate solutions like a slower cluster may be a good choice.

Summary of the Archive Pattern

The *Archive Pattern* targets reducing system costs more than improving performance. Financial and healthcare companies frequently use this pattern to satisfy government regulations. Operational data, like logs, rarely accessed as it ages, also benefit from this pattern.

Problem	• Some documents are used sparingly but must be kept for regulation purposes.
Solution	• Use different storage tiers. • Store older documents in a cheaper tier.
Use cases	• Financial applications. • Pharmaceuticals applications.
Benefits	• Reduces the costs of managing older documents. • Satisfies the regulatory requirements to keep data for an extended time.
Trade-offs	• Slower access to older documents. • The database management system may not support federated queries to all tiers together. • Changing the schema of archived documents may not be possible.

Table 13: The Archive Pattern.

The Attribute Pattern

Polymorphism is one of the most powerful attributes of the *Document Model*. It allows putting objects with different characteristics in one collection. But what if you can't predict the difference between objects and want to query these fields? In a traditional relational database, one would transpose or pivot a list of flexible attributes in a table and join them with the object ID. Each row has a foreign key to the main table, an attribute name, and its value. Can we do the same in MongoDB and avoid this unwanted join between two collections?

Overall description of the Attribute Pattern

The Attribute Pattern enables grouping multiple fields into a single index, making it possible to index fields whose key names are unknown at the time of index creation.

This pattern can benefit catalog applications where many fields describe a product. This pattern is also advantageous for conducting searches across these many fields.

MongoDB has a native functionality, *Wildcard Indexes*, that satisfies cataloging and search requirements by implementing a subcase of the *Attribute Pattern*. Another alternative to the *Attribute Pattern* is the *Atlas Search* functionality. The examples below will review both *Wildcard Indexes* and *Atlas Search* functionalities.

Let's start by reviewing the *Attribute Pattern*. Then using our example application use case, include an example utilizing the Wildcard Indexes functionality.

The *Attribute Pattern* has these variants:

- Using a key-value pair.
- Using a key-value pair and additional qualifiers.

Details of the Attribute Pattern

In a traditional relational database, we often represent an undefined list of columns for a given row as an attribute table. The attribute table is a pivot of the unpredictable columns. A one-to-many relationship exists between the original row and the attribute table.

When using this pattern, MongoDB uses a similar layout. The column for the name of the attributes becomes a field `"k": "field_name"`, while the column for the values becomes `"v": "value"`. The resulting document is more difficult to read and feels different than a usual JSON document.

The index is created as a combination of k and v with the following spec `{ "k": 1, "v":1 }`. The vital characteristic of this index is that it does not need to know the names of the attributes. They are not part of the index specification but are its values. The resulting index allows querying for attributes the schema is unaware of.

Implementing the Attribute Pattern

Take these steps to implement the *Attribute Pattern*:

- Identify the fields to gather together.

- Create an array that will contain these targeted fields.

- For each targeted field, create a subdocument in the array.

- For each subdocument, the target field's name becomes the value of k, while the value becomes the value of v.

- For additional qualifiers (q1, q2, …), an additional field should tie the values. The additional field should be consistent across most of the targeted fields.

- Create a compound index with all the fields k, v, q1, q2, …

For example, the fields representing the prices in the following document look initially like this.

```
{
    "_id": "12345",
    "name": "The Little Prince",
    ...
    "price_usa": Decimal(9.99)
    "price_france": Decimal(15.00)
}
```

Figure 64 shows the schema for the above document.

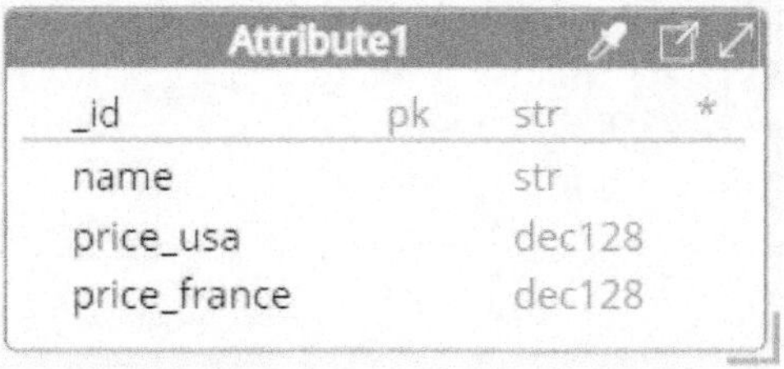

Figure 64: Attribute pattern schema example 1.

After applying the Attribute Pattern, they look like the following.

```
{
    "_id": "12345",
    "name": "The Little Prince",
    "prices": [
        {
            "k": "price_usa",
            "v": Decimal(9.99),
            "q": "USD"
        },
        {
            "k": "price_france",
            "v": Decimal(15.00),
            "q": "Euros"
        }
    ]
}
```

Figure 65 shows the schema for the above document.

Figure 65: Attribute pattern schema example 2.

Example of applying the Attribute Pattern with the pet adoption use case

We use the *Attribute Pattern* to model some fields we want to use to search for pets. We do not want to create an index for each newly added search criterion. The search page will have a drop-down menu for each search criterion. Use the wildcard index by grouping the attributes under a `details` field. The document may look as follows.

```
// a Pet document with attributes
{
    "_id": "bird102345",
    "pet_name": "Lady G",
    "details": [
        "character": "independent",
        "color": "green",
        "height": 0.2,          // 0.2 m or 20 cm
        "origin": "Venezuela",
        "voice": "marvelous",
        "weight": 0.3           // 0.3 kg or 300 g
    ]
}
```

The following statement would create the *Wildcard Index.*

```
db.pets.createIndex({ "details.$**": 1 });
```

Let's use the *Attribute Pattern* with a qualifier for the relationships between the keys and values. Pivoting the attributes gives us the following document.

```
// a Pet document with attributes
{
    "_id": "bird102345",
    "pet_name": "Lady G",
    "details": [
        { "k": "character", "v": "independent" },
        { "k": "color", "v": "green", "q": "dark" },
        { "k": "height", "v": 20, "q": "cm" },
        { "k": "origin", "v": "Venezuela" },
        { "k": "voice", "v": "marvelous" },
        { "k": "weight", "v": 300, "q": "g" }
    ]
}
```

Figure 66 shows the schema for the above document.

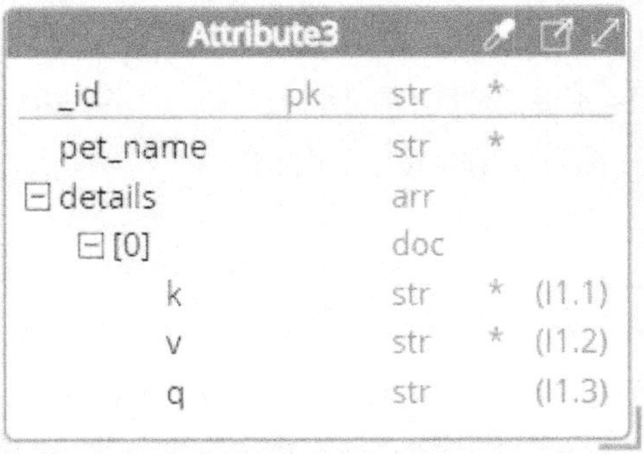

Attribute3				
_id	pk	str	*	
pet_name		str	*	
⊟ details		arr		
⊟ [0]		doc		
k		str	*	(I1.1)
v		str	*	(I1.2)
q		str		(I1.3)

Figure 66: Attribute pattern schema example 3.

Then, we create the following multi-key index.

```
db.pets.createIndex({ "details.k": 1, "details.v":1,
"details.q":1 });
```

The following query would find a pet that is dark green.

```
db.pets.find({ details: { $elemMatch: { "k": "color",
"v": "green", "q": "dark" }}});
```

Benefits of the Attribute Pattern

If we have too many indexes because of a large number of fields, this pattern will help lower the complexity and simplify the management of the database.

Instead of keeping an eye on new fields in the document to create additional indexes, the *Attribute Pattern* allows these new attributes to be added automatically as part of the index on all attributes in the group.

Trade-offs with the Attribute Pattern

The resulting representation of a document is less readable because the structure departs from the key/value representation used for the other parts of the document. In other words, the fields in this part of the document will look different from the other fields.

Furthermore, when querying with more than one field within the same subdocument, one must instruct MongoDB to use $elemMatch. Otherwise, querying on two fields without this keyword will return any document with a subdocument matching the first condition and a second document matching the second condition.

Summary of the Attribute Pattern

The *Attribute Pattern* allows indexing a set of fields at once. This ability is handy when there are unpredictable key names. It removes the difficulty in creating indexes on these unpredictable key names.

The *Wildcard Index* functionality in MongoDB has already codified a subset of this pattern. If the *Wildcard Index* functionality covers the application's needs, one should prefer it over implementing the *Attribute Pattern*.

Problem	• Many unpredictable keys in documents need to be indexed.
Solution	• Rearrange the fields as key-value pairs.
Use cases	• Product characteristics. • Set of fields with the same value type.
Benefits	• Lowers the number of indexes. • Allows considering new key names automatically by an index.
Trade-offs	• The pattern's k-v notation differs and is less readable than the other fields in the document. • The queries must use the $elemMatch operator between the field clauses.

Table 14: The Attribute Pattern.

The Bucket Pattern

In the early days of programming, one would feed a giant computer with punch cards. A separate card encoded each instruction. And yes, it was preferable not to drop the ordered stack of cards on the floor, especially if you did not use some labels to reorder them.

Just a little later, the advent of terminals permitted the developers to put all these instructions in a file. That was better. However, programs got bigger, and files got larger. Then, a single file was not a viable solution any longer.

The solution at that time was to group a set of instructions. Call it files, classes, or libraries; this is still the system in use today. The point we want to make is that sometimes, one needs a middle-of-the-road solution because both extremes are far from optimal. The punch card is too granular, while the "single file" solution is too broad and does not provide enough granularity.

Overall description of the Bucket Pattern

The *Bucket Pattern* is a solution between embedding a one-to-many relationship and keeping every object on the many sides in a separate document. It permits grouping the related documents in a more manageable size.

We often see the *Bucket Pattern* with Internet Of Things data, time series data, and any relationship with high cardinality. For example, one may want to group the measurements of a device or the revenues over a month for a given theater.

One may look into the native time series functionality of MongoDB. The implemented functionality is a subcase of the *Bucket Pattern*. The application will profit from many optimizations that MongoDB implements on the server side when using the functionality.

Details of the Bucket Pattern

By grouping individual pieces of information into buckets, we have documents with a predictable size optimized for the system.

One common quandary when applying this pattern is the amount of grouping that should be done. As said above, the resulting size of the document is one criterion.

Another critical question is how the application and the users will query the data later. For example, let's say an aggregation query is the most critical operation in terms of latency. If the query must start with an $unwind stage to expand the document, it indicates that the grouping is one more level than needed. To further illustrate the example, let's say the bucket for a document is a month of data. The most critical query needs to calculate daily averages from the values in the bucket to report these in the UI. Then this query tells us that a daily grouping may be more optimal.

When the workload has tight requirements for write and read operations, the solution may use a document with a bucket to capture the data at the proper grouping and another document in another collection to keep the data in a single document to speed up the read operations. The *Computed Pattern* is often used to precompute the operations on a bucket. In the example case above, the daily average could have been pre-calculated and stored in a bucket in another document.

Implementing the Bucket Pattern

To implement the *Bucket Pattern*, take the following steps:

- Identify the granularity of the bucket.

- Create an array to group the measurement or data.

- Identify a field at the document's root that identifies the bucket, like a date for time series data or a bucket number for entities bucketed by size.

Example of applying the Bucket Pattern with the pet adoption use case

On average, our pets get two to three interactions a week. Creating a document for each interaction seems excessive. On the other hand, putting all the interactions in the pet document will make archiving the documents a little more complicated than we want, so we will use the *Bucket Pattern* to model the interactions.

The first question relates to the granularity of the bucket. A week leads to very few observations per bucket, while a year may give too many and makes the archiving operation a little more complicated than needed. Hence, we settle for a granularity of the month.

Adding the measurements under the field `interactions` and identifying the bucket by the month in month, the documents in the interactions collection look like the following.

```
// an Interaction document with a bucket of
// monthly interactions
{
    "_id": {
        "pet_id": "bird102345",
        "month": ISODate("2023-02-01T00:00:00Z")
    },
    "interactions": [
        {
            "ts": ISODate("2023-02-14T22:14:00Z"),
            "userid": 34717
        },
        {
            "ts": ISODate("2023-02-15T20:00:00Z"),
            "userid": 31043
        },
        ...
    ]
}
```

Figure 67 shows the schema for the above document, in the ERD.

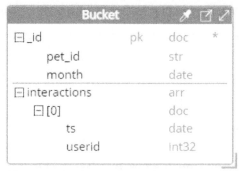

Figure 67: Bucket pattern schema example.

Figure 68 shows the schema tree view.

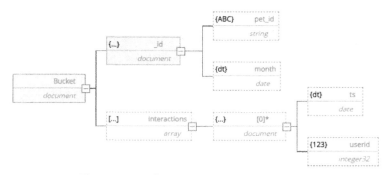

Figure 68: Bucket pattern schema tree view.

Benefits of the Bucket Pattern

If the *Bucket Pattern* groups what may have been separate documents, it reduces the number of read operations. On the other hand, if all data points were in one document, that single read may bring more information than needed in memory. The pattern may be a good compromise between the number of read operations and the amount of data read in memory.

The data is organized per unit of time, which makes it more manageable. One can compute summaries for the unit of time and store these computations in the document. For example, a monthly sum of the data stored in the document will make further aggregations faster; summing data for a year is a faster operation on the twelve partial sums than adding potentially thousands of documents every time.

It is easier to archive or delete a set of documents as long as they are a multiple of the grouping unit. For example, archiving three months of data when the grouping is by month is easy; however, archiving one week for documents containing one month of data is a little more complicated.

Another use case for the bucket pattern is to help page results. When displaying documents per page on a website, the application may issue new queries and ask to skip several documents. If the documents are organized per bucket, there are far fewer documents to read and skip.[7]

---

[7] See "Paging with the Bucket Pattern" by Justin LaBreck.
https://www.mongodb.com/blog/post/paging-with-the-bucket-pattern—part-1.

Trade-offs with the Bucket Pattern

Queries that operate on sections of a bucket are more challenging to write. Queries that need to unwind the elements of the array first before going further may suffer from performance versus simply adding values in documents.

The traditional BI tools may have difficulties operating on the elements of an array. MongoDB offers drivers to read from documents. However, one still needs to use array functions to manage the elements of a bucket.

Summary of the Bucket Pattern

The *Bucket Pattern* is an alternative to fully embedding or referencing relationships. It works best with one-to-many relationships. It is a pattern that requires a good understanding of the workload.

The Time Series functionality in MongoDB codifies the *Bucket Pattern* for its most common use case. The functionality also benefits from many performance implementations in the server. One should prefer this functionality if it satisfies the needs.

Problem	• Avoiding too many documents or documents too big. • A one-to-many relationship that can't be embedded.

Solution	• Define the optimal grouping of information. • Create an array to store the optimal amount per document.
Use cases	• Internet of Things. • Data Warehouse. • One-to-many relationships with high cardinality.
Benefits	• Provides a good balance between the number of read accesses and the size of the data returned. • Makes the data more manageable. • Easy to prune data. • Helps implement paging results.
Trade-offs	• Can lead to poor query results if not designed correctly. • Less friendly to BI tools.

Table 15: The Bucket Pattern.

The Computed Pattern

Some computations are expensive to do. Fortunately, computers are not as lazy as me. When tasked to redo the same task repeatedly, I want to automate it.

If one stores the information as base units in the database, the system may find itself redoing the exact computations, manipulations, or transformations over and over. With *Big Data* systems, these repeated computations can lead to poor performance.

Overall description of the Computed Pattern

The *Computed Pattern* allows faster read queries that would otherwise require complex computations. Typical computations are counters, roll-ups, sums, or other mathematical operations. The pattern is often seen in systems with higher performance requirements on read operations than write operations. IoT systems that report sums and averages over user-defined periods are good candidates for this pattern. In these systems, this pattern complements the *Bucket Pattern* or MongoDB native time series. The document contains a set of related data points and computations on the set. The *Computed Pattern* has the following variants:

- Counting and other mathematical operations.
- Rolling-up data.
- Fanning-out data.

Details of the Computed Pattern

The essence of the *Computed Pattern* is to compute something before it is needed. It usually makes sense to do it because there are many more read operations than write operations. Or the short required read latency makes running a computation on the data at read time prohibitive. In the case of more read operations than write operations, moving the computation during the write operation ensures we perform the computation less often. Also, this scenario does not produce any stale data.

In the case where there is a tight requirement on the read latency, we may have to settle for some data staleness. In this scenario, a periodic task produces the computations. However, the system may expose stale data between two job occurrences. As for any data anomaly, one must weigh the cost of doing these computations and showing stale data versus not meeting the latency requirement. For example, if a daily computation is calculating the product's popularity rank for the users, then the staleness is likely acceptable.

Once a computation completes, we should place the result in the document that has a one-to-one relationship with this computation. For example, we are using sales documents to compute the popularity of products. In that case, the resulting ranks have a one-to-one relationship with the product. We should put the resulting rankings in the product documents.

As for doing the subsequent computation, we can choose different strategies. The first is to keep the data source (details about the data) and re-run a whole computation. Another approach is to keep accumulators to perform the subsequent computation incrementally. In this latter case, we can delete the data source if desired. For example, when computing averages, keeping the sum and total with the average permits incrementally calculating the updated average values as more data points are available.

Variant A - Counting and other mathematical operations

This variant is the most common one. Systems with user interfaces often have to present data with counts and sums to give an overview of an object or trend. Showing this information quickly to the user is often more important than reporting the perfect numbers. Everything is relative; the offset should be manageable, so it leads to good decision-making from the system's end user.

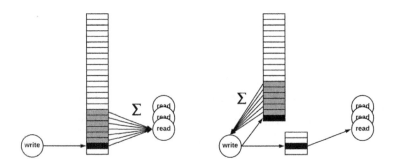

Figure 69: Computation examples.

Some examples of computations often seen in systems are:

- Counting, averaging, or summing observations in time series data.
- Ranking products, reviews, and comments.

Variant B - Rolling-up data

A data cube is a multi-dimensional array of values. Each array is a roll-up of data into a smaller piece of information. For example, we want to roll-up sales by region, dates, and product categories. When these roll-ups are too expensive to perform on the fly, using the *Computed Pattern* to prepare the data makes sense. Again, it compromises the acceptable staleness and the cost of performing the roll-ups at read time.

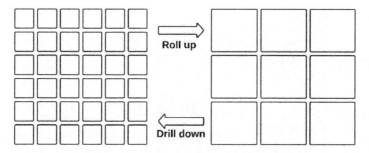

Figure 70: Roll up and drill down.

Variant C - Fanning-out data

The third variant is the opposite of the roll-up. In this variant, we duplicate the information to various sources, so each source does not have to gather the data. For example, in a social network application copying an image or text to all subscribers of a topic will save the read operation from assembling a page from many sources, rendering the user's page much quicker.

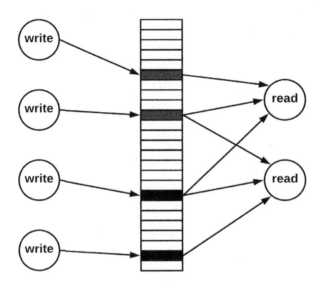

Figure 71: Scattered reads.

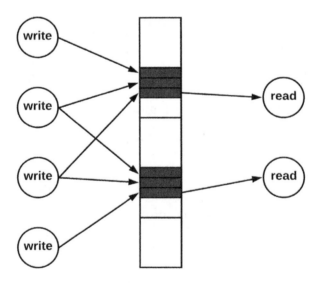

Figure 72: Preparing efficient reads at write time.

Implementing the Computed Pattern

To implement the *Computed Pattern*, take the following steps:

- Identify the too-frequent computation.

- Create a field in the document that has a one-to-one relationship to the computation to receive the results.

- Identify the frequency to perform the computation.

- Execute a script or trigger at the above frequency.

Example of applying the Computed Pattern with the pet adoption use case

In our Pet Adoption project, we will apply the *Computed Pattern* to calculate the interaction summary for the last three completed months. Alternatively, we could keep a rolling count over the previous 90 days, but it adds unneeded complexity, so the sum of the last three completed months is sufficient.

The computation result will go in the field `interactions_last_3_months` in the pets documents. We will compute the new values at the end of each month. An aggregation pipeline will update the values.

The modified pets documents look like the following.

```
// a Pet document with a sum of interactions for
// the last three completed months
{
    "_id": "bird102345",
    "pet_name": "Lady G",
    ...
    // Computed value from the interaction collection
    "interactions_last_3_months": 87
}
```

Figure 73 shows the schema for the above document.

Figure 73: Computed pattern schema example.

```
// Counting the number of interactions per pet
// for Jan, Feb, and March 2023
[
  {
    $match: {
      "_id.month": {
        $gte: ISODate("2023-01-01"),
        $lt: ISODate("2023-04-01"),
      },
    },
  },
  {
    $unwind: {
      path: "$interactions",
    },
  },
  {
    $group: {
      _id: "$_id.pet_id",
      sum: {
```

```
        $sum: 1,
      },
    },
  },
]
```

Benefits of the Computed Pattern

One of the main goals of the *Computed Pattern* is to make read operations faster. The read operation should be simpler and faster by pre-calculating data to be read beforehand.

When read operations are more common than the reads, a computation will likely be redone with the same data, providing the same results. We can avoid this by doing the computation with the write operation. Fewer computations translate to fewer CPU resources used.

Trade-offs with the Computed Pattern

The read operations may return stale data if the system can't recalculate the computations frequently enough. See our section on staleness for a complete discussion on the subject.

The computations may also produce data duplication. The calculations are simply a snapshot of other data at a given time.

Summary of the Computed Pattern

The *Computed Pattern* pre-computes data before the read operations to prevent longer retrieval times.

Problem	• Expensive computation or manipulation of data. • Computation executed frequently on the same data produces the same results.
Solution	• Execute the operation and store the result in the appropriate document either at write time or through a scheduler.
Use cases	• Internet of Things. • Event sourcing.
Benefits	• Read operations are faster. • Saving CPU and disk access resources.
Trade-offs	• Potentially creates staleness. • Potentially creates duplication of information.

Table 16: The Computed Pattern.

The Document Versioning Pattern

Most of you are familiar with Software Configuration Management Systems, also known as Source Code Control Systems or Version Control Systems. Tools like Git, ClearCase, Perforce, Mercurial, and CVS, let you keep a complete history of files, usually source code, so you go back to a previous state of your code base.

Or you may be more familiar with a *CMS* (Content Management System), which includes a similar functionality for keeping many revisions of your work.

These tools are powerful as they let your teams work concurrently on the same content and let you branch and merge work done on different streams. They do what they are supposed to do very well. If you need the full fledge of their power in your solution, you should use them.

At the other end of the spectrum, databases are very good at processing tons of queries and making frequent updates on the data; however, they usually can only represent the last state of the data.

So what happens if the application needs to refer to earlier versions of the documents?

You could use a database and an SCM. However, it makes the application more challenging to operate, as now you have to coordinate requests, operations, and backups across many systems.

Overall description of the Document Versioning Pattern

The *Document Versioning Pattern* is used to keep track of the changes in a document. This functionality is similar to Configuration Management Systems tracking changes to source code. Another analogy is the slow-changing dimensions (SCD) in data warehouses.

Regulated industries often use this pattern. Audits in sectors like banking and pharmaceuticals may need to look at older versions.

The *Document Versioning Pattern* has the following variants.

- Keeping all complete versions in a secondary collection.
- Storing only the differences between versions.

Details of the Document Versioning Pattern

The first variant is more straightforward if we want to look at the full documents, as the second variant needs to reconstruct versions based on differences. The simplicity of the first variant comes at the cost of using more storage for all revisions.

The second variant is more appropriate when many changes happen to documents, and the focus is on who made which change and when it occurred.

We will use the same example to demonstrate the two variants of this pattern.

Let's assume we are working with an insurance company with ten million customers. The company divides each customer policy into two parts. The first part is a standard policy, and the second part includes specific policy details for each customer, such as a list of all the add-ons to the standard policy and a list of specific insured items. We need the history of modifications to that list for either regulatory purposes or to combat fraud. So, we want to track any changes to the custom lists.

Going back to our list of requirements, we have ten million customers, each has about one modification per year, and 99.9% of the queries are about the current policy, so this should be a perfect use case for the pattern.

The first variant works better if only a few versions exist for a given document. We prefer the second variant when tracking frequent changes per document.

Variant A - Keeping all complete versions in a secondary collection

There should be a few documents to version for the first variant. The more documents we have, the lower average of revisions we should have. The product of the number of documents by the average number of revisions should be manageable by our hardware resources. Having hundreds of revisions for a billion documents may be challenging to manage.

The first variant of this pattern works if we frequently query the last revision of each document. The pattern optimizes the schema, so all the queries reading from the latest version do not suffer from any performance impact.

We will create two collections for the parts-specific customers. The first collection, `cust_policies_rev`, keeps all the revisions of all documents. The second collection, `cust_policies`, saves one revision per customer, the latest.

Let's say one customer just acquired a ring and wants to add it to their policy. We create a new document revision. The document will be the previous revision, to which we applied the modifications for this customer. We write the document into the collection `cust_policies_rev`, which has all the documents' revisions. Then we write the same document as an update to the previous current revision for this document in the collection `cust_policies`, which only contains the *latest* revision of the documents. Keeping only the latest revisions in the collection can keep the queries simple and performant. There is no need to go through hoops to select only the latest revision of a document.

In our example, we insert the following document into the `cust_policies` collection.

```
// the first revision/version of the specific clauses
// for a given document
{
    "customer_id": "568903845",
    "revision": 1,
    "ts": "2023-03-01 15:15:15",
    "name": "Daniel Coupal",
    "insured_items": [
        { "type": "home", "address": ... },
        { "type": "life", "age": ...}
    ],
    ...
}
```

Figure 74 shows the schema for the above document.

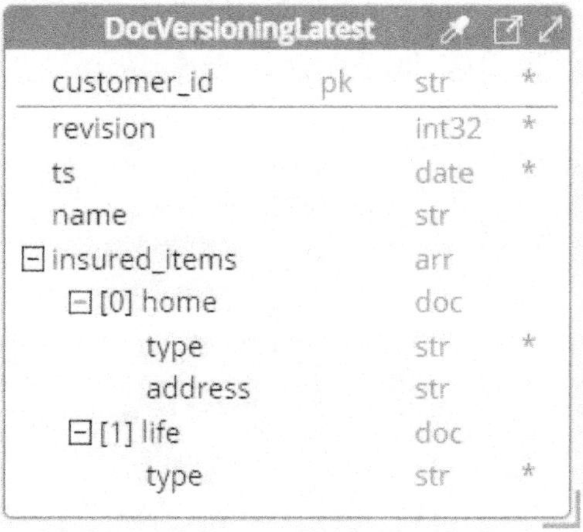

DocVersioningLatest			
customer_id	pk	str	*
revision		int32	*
ts		date	*
name		str	
⊟ insured_items		arr	
⊟ [0] home		doc	
type		str	*
address		str	
⊟ [1] life		doc	
type		str	*

Figure 74: Document versioning schema example 1.

We also insert the document into the `cust_policies_rev` collection. Later, when the customer wants to add a ring, we add the item to the document, as shown here:

```
// the first revision/version of the specific clauses
// for a given document
{
    "customer_id": "568903845",
    "revision": 1,
    "ts": "2023-04-01 16:16:16",
    "name": "Daniel Coupal",
    "insured_items": [
      { "type": "home", "address": ... },
      { "type": "life", "age": ... },
      { "type": "jewelry", "desc": "ring", ... }
    ],
    ...
}
```

Figure 75 shows the schema for the above document.

DocVersioningRev			
customer_id	pk	str	*
revision		int32	*
ts		date	*
name		str	
⊟ insured_items		arr	
⊟ [0] home		doc	
type		str	*
address		str	
⊟ [1] life		doc	
type		str	*
⊟ [2] jewelry		doc	
type		str	*
description		str	

Figure 75: Document versioning schema example 2.

We update the document in the `cust_policies` collection by searching by `customer_id`. And we insert the document in the `cust_policies_rev` collection. Note that inserting the document in the second collection requires removing the primary key of the document `_id`. MongoDB will add an auto-generated primary key (`_id`) if the document to insert does not have one. With this variant, we may consider keeping only some of the revisions, but only the last X revisions or those less than X days or years.

Variant B - Storing only the differences between versions

In the second variant, we store only the differences between versions. We can keep these differences in the document if they represent a small or manageable size. Alternatively, if the list of modifications is too long, we store the differences in a different collection. Using the same scenario as the first variant, the first revision of the document looks like the following.

```
// the first revision/version of the specific clauses
// for a given document
{
    "customer_id": "568903845",
    "revision": 1,
    "creation_ts": "2023-03-01 15:15:15",
    "last_update_ts": "2023-03-01 15:15:15",
    "name": "Daniel Coupal",
    "insured_items": [
        { "type": "home", "address": ... },
        { "type": "life", "age": ...}
    ],
    ...
}
```

Figure 76 shows the schema for the above document.

DocVersioningLatestVarB			
customer_id	pk	str	*
revision		int32	*
creation_ts		date	*
last_update_ts		date	
name		str	*
⊟ insured_items		arr	
⊟ [0] home		doc	
type		str	*
address		str	
⊟ [1] life		doc	
type		str	*

Figure 76: Document versioning schema example 3.

The following document revision tracks the deltas between our revisions. In this case, we keep all documents in only one collection.

```
// the second revision/version of the specific
// clauses for a given document
{
    "customer_id": "568903845",
    "revision": 2,
    "creation_ts": "2023-03-01 15:15:15",
    "last_update_ts": "2023-04-01 16:16:16",
    "name": "Daniel Coupal",
    "insured_items": [
        { "type": "home", "address": ... },
        { "type": "life", "age": ...},
        { "type": "jewelry", "desc": "ring", ... }
    ],
    "changes": [
        { "revision": 2,
          "ts": "2023-04-01 16:16:16",
          "user": "Ins Agento",
          "change_field": "insured_items",
          "action": "add",
          "what": { "type": "jewelry",
```

```
                    "desc": "ring", ... }
        }
    ]
    ...
}
```

Figure 77 shows the schema for the above document.

DocVersioningRevVarB			
customer_id	pk	str	*
revision		int32	*
creation_ts		date	*
last_update_ts		date	
name		str	*
⊟ insured_items		arr	
⊟ [0] home		doc	
type		str	*
address		str	
⊟ [1] life		doc	
type		str	*
⊟ [2] jewelry		doc	
type		str	
description		str	
⊟ changes		arr	
⊟ [0]		doc	
revision		str	*
ts		date	*
user		str	*
action		str	*
⊟ what		doc	
type		str	*
description		str	

Figure 77: Document versioning schema example 4.

To have a readable format of a previous version, we must reconstruct that version from the deltas. This operation adds complexity to the code that we would avoid with the first variant.

Other variants

A third variant is to keep all versions in one collection and have a flag to identify the *latest* version. The main problems with this variant are that it does not reduce the collection size, and all queries must ensure they specify that they want to use the latest version. Additionally, using an index for selecting and sorting becomes more challenging to manage correctly.

Implementing the Document Versioning Pattern

To implement the *Document Versioning Pattern*, take the following steps:

- Add a field to keep track of the version number.

- Add a creation date for the version.

- Identify a second collection or other storage to receive older or all document versions.

- For the variant that keeps complete versions, modify the code to update the main collection with the latest version and insert the new version in the location that supports all versions.

- Segregate code that looks for the latest version versus looking for an older version.

Example of applying the Document Versioning Pattern with the pet adoption use case

The Document Versioning Pattern will fulfill the requirement of keeping track of any changes to the pet adoption certificates.

Here is an example of an adoption certificate document:

```
// an adoption Certificate document with
// Document Versioning
{
    "pet_id": "dog100666",
    "revision": 1,
    "last_update": "2023-01-06",
    "pet_name": "Cujo",
    "adoption_date": "2023-01-08",
    "new_owners": [ "Steve King" ],
    "clauses": [
      "Adoption center will vaccinate dog for flu"
    ]
    ...
}
```

Figure 78 shows the schema for the above document.

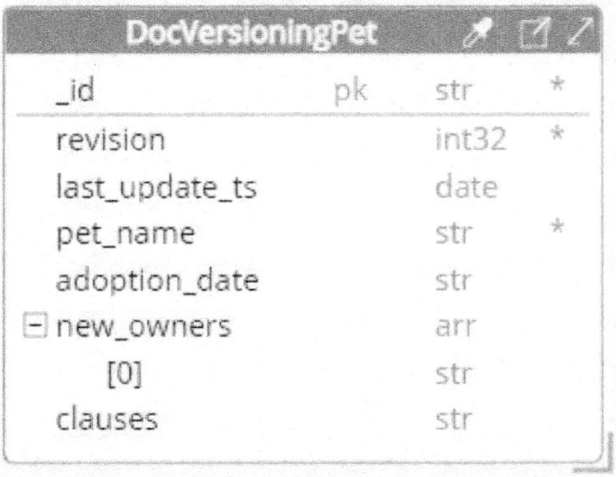

Figure 78: Document versioning pet schema example 1.

Then the new owners request to add Carrie, the family's daughter, as an owner on the certificate and convince the center to provide six months of special food for Cujo, who is just coming out of an illness. With these changes, the new version of the adoption certificate may look like this:

```
// an adoption Certificate document with
// Document Versioning
{
    "pet_id": "dog100666",
    "revision": 2,
    "last_update": "2023-01-07",
    "pet_name": "Cujo",
    "adoption_date": "2023-01-08",
    "new_owners": [ "Steve King", "Carrie King" ],
    "clauses": [
      "Adoption center will vaccinate dog for flu",
      "Adoption center will provide six months of
special dog food"
    ]
    ...
}
```

The schema remains the same, as shown in Figure 79

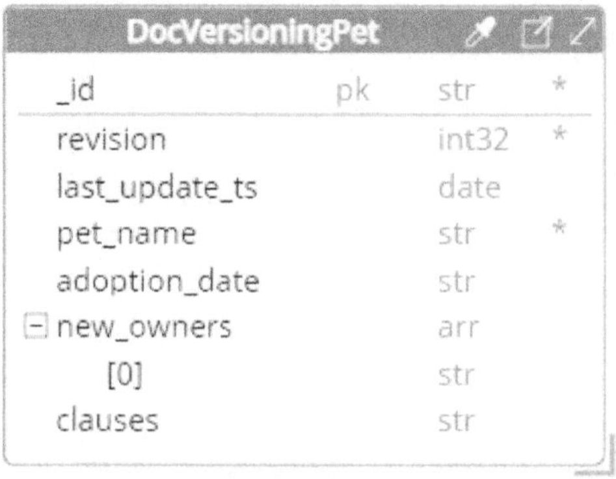

Figure 79: Document versioning pet schema example 2.

From a system perspective, this new revision of the adoption certificate is the one that the system will always pull. We keep this revision in an `adoption_certificates` collection. However, because there is a requirement to track the history of the certificate, we will also keep the previous versions in a separate collection, `previous_adoption_certificate`.

When updating the certificate, the system would run the following queries.

```
// Here, we replace the whole document,
// but $set may be more appropriate
// for small updates on a large document
db.adoption_certificate.updateOne({"pet_id":
"dog10666"}, new_certificate_doc)

db.previous_adoption_certificate.insert(new_certifica
te_doc)
```

Note that the documents can not use the `pet_id` as the `_id` because we allow many documents per pet in the `previous_adoption_certificate` collection. In this case, not providing an _id field will result in MongoDB adding one with an `ObjectId()` type.

At this point, the `previous_adoption_certificate` would have two documents for Cujo. We retrieve the documents with the following query.

```
db.previous_adoption_certificate.find({"pet_id":
"dog10666"})
```

Benefits of the Document Versioning Pattern

Unless the documents we need to version have a high rate of changes, there is little overhead in managing them with the *Document Versioning Pattern*. Replace the updates with an update and an insert statement. One may want to wrap the two operations in a transaction to ensure consistency.

Trade-offs with the Document Versioning Pattern

For documents with a high rate of changes, doubling the number of writes may be significant. When making a full copy of the document, it is easier to compare the documents; however, it consumes more space. On huge documents, it may be significant.

With many versions available, the system may need extra capabilities to show differences and manage older versions.

Summary of the Document Versioning Pattern

The *Document Versioning Pattern* permits avoiding a configuration management system to track changes. It also helps audits to identify when and how documents changed.

Problem	• Need to keep older versions of the documents. • Do not want to use a separate system (SCM or CMS) to keep track of a few document changes.

Solution	• Use a field to track the version number of the document. • Use separate collections to keep the latest and older documents.
Use cases	• Financial applications. • Insurance applications. • Legal documents. • Price or product description histories.
Benefits	• Little performance impact of keeping older versions.
Trade-offs	• Doubles the number of write operations. • Frequent updates on large documents will consume more disk space. • Read operations must target the right collection containing either the latest or all the documents.

Table 17: The Document Versioning Pattern.

The Envelope Pattern

The purpose of the *Envelope Pattern* is to separate data intended for consumption (the "payload"), from data intended to optimize the power and flexibility of the database and application (the "envelope".) It can be used to harmonize data for more complete indexing and query results, track lineage, and more.

There are several justifications to group envelope and payload in separate sections of a document. Maybe parts of the document must be kept in sync with legacy systems. Maybe you need to standardize some data in a canonical form. Maybe you want just a cleaner organization inside your documents. This *Envelope Pattern* can be combined with one or more patterns reviewed in this section, including the *Schema Versioning Pattern* and the *Inheritance Pattern*.

Overall description of the Envelope Pattern

The basic idea is to create a structure for the document that contains two distinct parts:

- The "envelope": this part wraps metadata like version numbers, timestamps, lineage, harmonized information, or other data used for indexing or other database operations,

- The "payload": this part contains the actual data intended to be consumed by the application.

Details of the Envelope Pattern

With JSON and the MongoDB document model, it is easy to create logical groups of information and organize documents in a friendly manner, not just for humans but also for systems. The naming of each group is not particularly important, as long as it is consistent and meaningful to your organization. For example, the "envelope" can also be called "header" or "metadata". Whereas the "payload" could also be called "data" or "instance". As a matter of fact, you could also decide that the "payload" does not need to be nested in its own object and prefer to keep it at the root level of the document.

```
// a document with an envelope for metadata
// separate from the data payload
{
    "_id": "bird102345",
    "header": {
        "schema_version": 4,
        "docRevision": 1,
        "creation_ts": "2023-03-01 15:15:15",
        "last_update_ts": "2023-03-01 15:15:15",
        "created_by": "jdoe",
        "provenance": {
            "source": "System A",
        },
        "lineage": "map v0.1.3",
        "harmonization": {
            "zipcode": "29466-0317",
        },
        "phone": "+1-555-444-7890"
    },
    "related_to": [],
    "payload": { ... }
}
```

Figure 80 shows the schema for the above example.

In this example, the metadata is grouped under a "header" subobject, while the data is in a "payload" subobject. In this example of metadata, there is a subobject for lineage, a subobject for harmonization of data, and a subobject used in the context of the *Single Collection Pattern*, which is detailed later in the schema design patterns section.

Figure 80: Envelope pattern schema example 1.

The harmonization section could be used, for example, if data in this collection comes from different legacy systems. There could be a case when address data uses different field names for the same information: zip, postcode, postal_code, etc. We assume here that there's a good reason to keep the field names in their original version, hence using a harmonization section to ensure compatibility.

Implementing the Envelope Pattern

To implement the *Envelope Pattern*, take the following steps:

- Split the fields of your document into an "envelope" group and a "payload" group, according to the nature of the information.

- Add the logic in the application code to handle lineage, harmonization, and other metadata fields, if applicable.

- Optionally migrate old documents to the new structure.

Example of applying the Envelope Pattern with the pet adoption use case

Applying the *Envelope Pattern* is very easy, and it can be combined with all the other schema design patterns covered in this section. The only difficulty might be in migrating to this pattern if you did not adopt it from the start. With our Pet system, as originally imagined, data has been coming from a single Access database. But we can imagine that business has been booming, and our animal shelter has acquired a competitor across town. We now have to integrate data from multiple systems, and of course, different naming conventions and formats have been used. During the transition period, we must ensure compatibility with the different systems.

```
// a document coming from the animal
// shelter's Access database
{
    "_id": "bird102345",
    "header": {
        "schema_version": 2,
        "docRevision": 1,
        "creation_ts": "2023-03-01 15:15:15",
        "last_update_ts": "2023-03-01 15:15:15",
        "created_by": " John Smith ",
        "provenance": {
            "source": "MS-Access",
            "lineage": " map v0.2.2"
        },
        "harmonization": {
            "zipcode": "74866-3457",
            "phone": "+1-555-444-7890"
        },
        "related_to": []
    },
    "payload": {
        "new_owner": "Steve King",
        "phoneNumber": "555-444-7890",
        "full_address": {
            "houseNum": "74866",
            "street": "123 Main Street",
            "box": "Apt. 749",
            "city": "Anytown",
            "state": "CA",
            "zip": "29466-0317"
        }
    }
```

```
}

// a document coming from the acquired
// competitor's Database
{
    "_id": "dog980453",
    "header": {
        "schema_version": 4,
        "docRevision": 1,
        "creation_ts": "2023-03-01 15:15:15",
        "last_update_ts": "2023-03-01 15:15:15",
        "created_by": "jdoe",
        "provenance": {
            "source": "System D",
            "lineage": "map v0.1.3"
        },
        "harmonization": {
            "zipcode": "74962-1347",
            "phone": "+1-555-444-7890"
        },
        "related_to": []
    },
    "payload": {
        "name": "Ella Goodson",
        "homephone": "555-444-7890",
        "address": "3780 Old House Drive",
        "city": "Worthington",
        "state": "MD",
        "postal": "74962"
    }
}
```

The schema for the above documents appears in Figure 81.

Figure 81: Envelope pattern schema example 2.

You will notice that this *Envelope Pattern* example also uses the *Schema Versioning Pattern* and the *Inheritance Pattern* to accommodate the different structures of the two source systems.

With Hackolade Studio, you can prefill each new document schema in your model with the structure of your choice using the Snippets functionality.

Benefits of the Envelope Pattern

Separating metadata from the payload can help with the efficiency and accuracy of queries and other database operations. This is achieved by harmonizing data coming from different systems at the time of creation of the document, so each query can be trusted to return accurate results without altering data that might be necessary for legacy systems.

The grouping of information can also help with the legibility and understanding of documents. Finally, the *Envelope Pattern* can be used for special indexing needs and in the context of the *Single Collection Pattern*.

Trade-offs with the Envelope Pattern

The additional metadata in the envelope can add some complexity to the data model and APIs. Depending on the application, the benefits might be minimal and not worth the complexity.

In some circumstances, separating the metadata from the payload may actually make queries less efficient, for example, if the metadata needs to be joined with the payload to produce the expected result.

Summary of the Envelope Pattern

Problem	• Data stored with different structures must be queried in a uniform manner.
Solution	• Separate data intended for consumption (the "payload"), from data intended to optimize the power and flexibility of the database and application (the "envelope".).
Use cases	• Data lineage. • Integration of data coming from different legacy systems.
Benefits	• Improve the efficiency and accuracy of queries by harmonizing data at document creation time. • Improve legibility and understanding of documents by grouping metadata and data payload separately.
Trade-offs	• Increased complexity of document structure and APIs. • Potentially makes queries less efficient, if metadata must be joined with the payload.

Table 18: The Envelope Pattern.

The Extended Reference Pattern

Even if you migrated from a ten tables relational model in a traditional relational database to a three collections model in MongoDB, you might still find yourself doing a lot of queries that need to join data from different collections.

The MongoDB queries are more straightforward than the corresponding SQL queries. Still, in the *Big Data* world, anything executed often can become a liability for performance, especially joins.

Overall description of the Extended Reference Pattern

The *Extended Reference Pattern* is an alternate solution between embedding and linking another document. It embeds the frequently used section of the document to avoid doing joins for important queries. And it keeps a complete version of the document in another location, referencing it when we need more information.

This pattern helps meet performance requirements for many applications. The typical use case is the need to model many-to-many relationships where embedding the full document leads to data duplication. For example, one can extract the required customer, product, or account characteristics and place this information in the parent document.

If no set of fields satisfies the application of this pattern, the *Single Collection Pattern* may be the right solution.

Details of the Extended Reference Pattern

Queries in a traditional relational database aggregate part of rows together through references using joins. As discussed earlier, joins are expensive and should be avoided when designing with a document database.

To avoid doing a join, you can embed with MongoDB. However, there are situations where embedding could be more problematic. For example, for many-to-many relationships, embedding brings data duplication.

Using our Movie Database as an example, let's assume we want to create an application focusing on movies (as opposed to focusing on actors). One possible design may be to have one collection for the movies and a different collection for the actors instead of embedding the actors into the movies in one collection. This two collections design allows a simple update to an actor document when something related to an actor changes; however, a join will be necessary between the two collections for most queries.

Using the Extended Reference Pattern, you can prevent having to perform a join and still have the information in two different documents. Instead of having a simple actorID as a reference, we will extend this reference by adding more fields, for example, the actor name. This design allows displaying a movie with all the actors by simply retrieving the movie document.

Another example of when to utilize the Extended Reference Pattern is in applications regarding orders and customers. If we center the system around the orders, we have a one-to-many relationship with the customers. To avoid duplicating everything about the customers, we may embed the customer's name, telephone number, and address into the order. If there is a need to get more information about the customer, a query will retrieve the complete document for the given customer.

When choosing which fields to augment the information of the reference, opt for fields that do not change or rarely change. In our examples above, the actor's name is a stable value. The same applies to the customer's name who passed a specific order.

Hackolade describes this concept of bringing additional fields from one entity to another as a *Foreign Master* in *Hackolade Studio*. The tool also reflects the information in the Document Relationship Diagrams.

Implementing the Extended Reference Pattern

To implement the *Extended Reference Pattern*, take the following steps:

- Identify frequent queries where it is possible to avoid joins.

- Copy the fields from the references into the main document.

- Align the source code to update changes in the data source and the extended references, or use change streams to apply changes when they happen.

Example of applying the Extended Reference Pattern with the pet adoption use case

In our original model for the Pet Adoption application, we already use the *Extended Reference Pattern*. We store the reference to the breed codes and the breed names for a given pet. Similarly, we do the same for the colors and vaccinations. These three pieces of information are all examples of using the *Extended Reference Pattern*.

The purpose of storing the code and the name is two-fold. When displaying a pet, we also want to show the breed list. If we only had the breed code (a foreign key to the breed collections), we must join the breed table with a join like for a traditional relational database. As we have seen a few times in this book, *joins* are expensive, and we must avoid them for a system to perform well. So instead of only storing the reference to the other table, we include the most frequently used information, in this case, the breed name. The breed code is still helpful for pulling more information about the breed if a user requests it by clicking on the breed name. In other words, as described earlier, copy in the fields for frequent queries to avoid performing joins.

```
// a Breed document
{
    "_id": "breed101",
    "name": "Dalmatian",
    "origin": "Croatia",
    "traits": [
        "loyal to the family",
        "good with children",
        ...
    ],
    ...
}

// a Pet document
{
    "_id": "dog19370824",
    "name": "Fanny",
    "breeds": [
        {
            "code": "breed101",
            "name": "Dalmatian"
        }
    ]
}
```

Figure 82 shows the schema for the documents above.

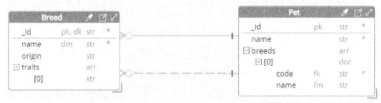

Figure 82: Extended reference pattern schema example.

The last thing to comment on for this example is that the breed name is usually immutable. However, when renaming a breed, the system should also rename the strings for each pet with this breed in its list. The documentation of *Foreign Masters* in the data model helps keep track of the fields that need updating when the data in the master parent collection changes.

Benefits of the Extended Reference Pattern

Because the *Extended Reference Pattern* represents a pre-joined relationship, reads will be faster. There is no need to open two cursors and perform two read operations. The document contains all the data.

Without applying the *Extended Reference Pattern*, we could have joined either by a $lookup, reading many documents from different collections, or using the *Single Collection Pattern*. Using the *Extended Reference Pattern* avoided joins, saving a lot of resources.

Trade-offs with the Extended Reference Pattern

Maintaining more information than a simple reference to another object means we will duplicate information. This duplication comes at a cost; but can also be minimal if the additional fields are not mutable values.

Summary of the Extended Reference Pattern

The *Extended Reference Pattern* is a good solution when embedding and referencing are not optimal. It works well for modeling many-to-many relationships.

Problem	• Too many joins in read operations. • Embedding leads to documents that are too big.
Solution	• Identify fields using joins for the most common read operations. • Copy these fields as an embedded subdocument in the main document.
Use cases	• Catalog. • Mobile applications. • Real-time analytics.
Benefits	• Faster reads. • Lesser number of joins and lookups.
Trade-offs	• Potentially creates data duplication.

Table 19: The Extended Reference Pattern.

The Graph Pattern

We have a project that needs to do much with the data, like search text descriptions, establish oriented relationships between objects, and many high-velocity queries. Let's use the best of each breed, a graph database, a search database, and obviously MongoDB for our project. This solution looks cool to software engineers, but the operation team will despise them.

If the application needs many systems, so be it. However, if some specialized requirements are less critical, one should consider using fewer database systems. MongoDB shines by offering some built-in functionality to cover some graph functionalities.

This section describes how the *Graph Pattern* can represent graphs in non-graph databases and use MongoDB to help traverse the graphs.

Overall description of the Graph Pattern

The *Graph Pattern* permits graph operations between documents. It allows designing an application with MongoDB as its unique database, no longer having to sync the information to a native graph database for additional functions.

Applications requiring document database functionality and graph processing capabilities can benefit from this pattern. For example, a system representing relationships between people and banking transactions may need these for fraud investigations.

If the relationship queries are not deep and performance is essential, one may want to use the *Single Collection Pattern*.

The *Graph Pattern* has the following variants.

- Referencing the outgoing edges (children).
- Referencing the incoming edges (parents).
- Referencing all edges.

Details of the Graph Pattern

Graphs can be directed or undirected. In the case of directed graphs, each node has a list of parents (incoming edges) and children (outgoing edges). In the case of an undirected graph, each node has a list of connections (edges).

When modeling a directed graph, one can model only one side of the relationships. This more straightforward representation requires knowing the start of the graph and constantly traversing the graph in only one direction. The advantage of modeling only one side of the relationship is to avoid data duplication.

When representing both sides, two nodes describe the edge between them; it is necessary to update both nodes for consistency. To illustrate the variants, we will use the following graph in Figure 83.

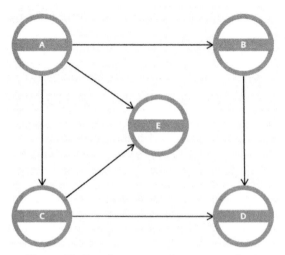

Figure 83: Graph pattern schema example 1.

This graph is "cyclic" because it contains at least one cycle (A ⇒ C ⇒ E ⇒ A). One needs to handle "cyclic" graphs carefully when using any recursion to traverse them.

To handle cyclic graphs in MongoDB, use the $lookup aggregation stage. This stage has a maxDepth parameter to avoid recursion or traversing too many levels in the graph.

Variant A - Referencing the outgoing edges (children)

This variant applies to directed graphs. Let's model our graph with only the children's relationship. The modeled documents look like the following.

```
{ "_id": "A", "children" : [ "B", "C" ] },
{ "_id": "B", "children" : [ "D" ] },
{ "_id": "C", "children" : [ "D", "E" ] },
{ "_id": "D", "children" : [ ] },
{ "_id": "E", "children" : [ "A" ] }
```

The schema for the above documents appears in Figure 84.

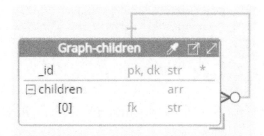

Figure 84: Graph pattern schema example 2.

The following aggregation query will retrieve all descendants for each node.

```
db.pattern_graph_children.aggregate([
  {
    $graphLookup:
      {
        from: "pattern_graph_children",
        startWith: "$children",
        connectFromField: "children",
        connectToField: "_id",
        as: "descendants",
        maxDepth: 20,
      },
  },
])
```

By adding a { $match: { "_id": "A" } } filter as the first stage of the aggregation, we can also limit the traversal to one node by specifying it as the only node to find descendants.

Variant B - Referencing the incoming edges (parents)

This variant applies to directed graphs. Let's model our graph with only the parent's relationship. The modeled documents look like the following.

```
{ "_id": "A", "parents" : [ "E" ] },
{ "_id": "B", "parents" : [ "A" ] },
{ "_id": "C", "parents" : [ "A" ] },
{ "_id": "D", "parents" : [ "B", "C" ] },
{ "_id": "E", "parents" : [ "C" ] }
```

The schema for the above documents appears in Figure 85.

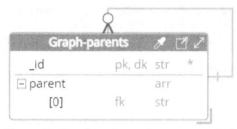

Figure 85: Graph pattern schema example 3.

The following aggregation query will retrieve all descendants for each node.

```
db.pattern_graph_parents.aggregate([
  {
    $graphLookup:
      {
        from: "pattern_graph_parents",
        startWith: "$parents",
        connectFromField: "parents",
        connectToField: "_id",
        as: "ancestors",
        maxDepth: 20,
      },
  },
])
```

Variant C - Referencing all edges

The referencing all edges variant models both sides of the edges. This variant gives more flexibility to graph traversals; however, it requires the update of two nodes when a relationship is added or removed.

We have the following model for an oriented graph using the "referencing all the edges" variant.

```
{"_id":"A", "parents":["E"], "children":["B", "C"]},
{"_id":"B", "parents":["A"], "children":["D"]},
{"_id":"C", "parents":["A"], "children":["D", "E"]},
{"_id":"D", "parents":["B", "C"], "children":[ ]},
{"_id":"E", "parents":["C"], "children":["A"]}
```

The schema for the above documents appears in Figure 86.

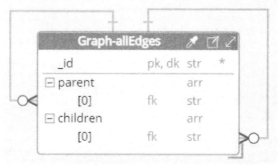

Figure 86: Graph pattern schema example 4.

While we model the unoriented graph with the following.

```
{ "_id": "A", "edges" : [ "B", "C", "E" ] },
{ "_id": "B", "edges" : [ "A", "D" ] },
{ "_id": "C", "edges" : [ "A", "D", "E" ] },
{ "_id": "D", "edges" : [ "B", "C" ] },
{ "_id": "E", "edges" : [ "A", "C" ] }
```

The schema for the above documents appears in Figure 87.

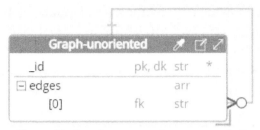

Figure 87: Graph pattern schema example 5.

One can traverse the complete graph through the edges from node "A" with the following query.

```
[
  {
    $match:
      {
        _id: "A",
      }
  },
  {
    $graphLookup:
      {
        from: "pattern_graph_edges",
        startWith: "$edges",
        connectFromField: "edges",
        connectToField: "_id",
        as: "connections",
        maxDepth: 10
      },
  },
]
```

Implementing the Graph Pattern

To implement the *Graph Pattern*, take the following steps.

- Identify which variant best balances performance and overhead for data duplication.

- Create a field containing references to linked nodes for a non-directed graph or two fields to keep track of ancestors and descendants in an oriented graph.

- Create a script or a trigger to update the dependencies when needed.

Example of applying the Graph Pattern with the pet adoption use case

One of our requirements for our Pet Adoption use case is to track the information about the mother and father of our pets. We could use the *Tree Pattern* if we only kept track of the mother and the mother's mother (grandmother) and so on. However, in this use case, we assume that we have data regarding the father in some occurrences, and we also want to track it. We must model the ancestry with a graph because a node (pet) may have two identified parents. We will model the relationships with a directed graph to preserve the parent-child information.

```
// some Pet documents
// Fanny
{
    "_id": "dog19370824",
    "name": "Fanny",
    "sex": "female",
    "relatives": {
        "mother": "dog19350224",
        "father": "dog19360824"
    }
},
// Fanny's mother
{
```

```
    "_id": "dog19350224",
    "name": "Perdita",
    "sex": "female",
    "relatives": {
        // No info. She was a rescued dog
    }
},
// Fanny's father
{
    "_id": "dog19360824",
    "name": "Pongo",
    "sex": "male",
    "relatives": {
        // No info. He was a rescued dog
    }
},
// Fanny's first child
{
    "_id": "dog20200110",
    "name": "Finn",
    "sex": "female",
    "relatives": {
        "mother": "dog19370824"
    }
},
// Fanny's second child
{
    "_id": "dog20201206",
    "name": "Canuck",
    "sex": "male",
    "relatives": {
        "mother": "dog19370824"
    }
}
```

The schema for the above documents appears in Figure 88.

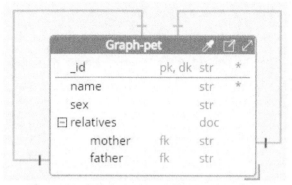

Figure 88: Graph pattern schema example 6.

We can find Fanny's children by looking at the documents that include her as a mother.

```
db.pets.find({"relatives.mother":"dog19370824"})
```

Trying to find all the descendants of Fanny becomes a little more complicated. It would be simpler to traverse the graph down through the children, so we may want to add a field to track the children. We now have data duplication; however, this anomaly is maintenance-free as this parent-child relationship does not change over time.

```
// Fanny with an array of her children
{
    "_id": "dog19370824",
    "name": "Fanny",
    "relatives": {
        "mother": "dog19350224",
        "father": "dog19360824",
        "children": [ "dog20200110", "dog20201206"]
    }
},
```

The schema for the above document appears in Figure 89.

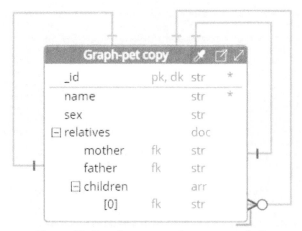

Figure 89: Graph pattern schema example 7.

Using the `$graphLookup` functionality of MongoDB, we can find all descendants of each pet with the following query.

```
db.pet.aggregate([
    {
        "$graphLookup": {
            "from": "pet",
            "startWith": "$relatives.children",
            "connectFromField": "relatives.children",
            "connectToField": "_id",
            "as": "descendants",
            // limit the recursion in case we have
            // bad circular links in the dataset
            "maxDepth": 10
        },
    },
])
```

Benefits of the Graph Pattern

If graph requirements are few, avoid using an additional graphing database system using the model-directed relationships between objects in MongoDB. The complexity of deploying this pattern within the solution will make the overall system more manageable over time.

Trade-offs with the Graph Pattern

`$graphLookup` is costly because of the join operations it performs. We should avoid it on high-frequency or low-latency queries.

Another concern is that variants using deeper than one-level relationships create duplication of information. For example, a connection from A to B to C duplicates a connection to C in the B object. If the connection changes, we need to modify a few documents. Bidirectional relationships, like A pointing to B and B pointing to A, also potentially create an integrity issue, as we can't delete only one of the two links.

Summary of the Graph Pattern

The *Graph Pattern* allows modeling a graph relationship between objects without using a separate graph database.

Problem	• The application needs graph operations as a lesser requirement.
Solution	• Reference one or a combination of parents, child, and ancestor documents.
Use cases	• People relationships. • Any graph relationships.

Benefits	• Avoid using a separate database system for a few graph operations.
Trade-offs	• $graphLookup is a costly join operation. • Potentially creates data duplication.

Table 20: The Graph Pattern.

The Inheritance Pattern

We used to call this pattern the *Polymorphic Pattern*. With the emergence of the *Single Collection Pattern* in our design, we renamed this pattern and instead used "polymorphism" as a category for classifying patterns.

Overall description of the Inheritance Pattern

The *Inheritance Pattern* permits the storage of documents that share a set of fields used for queries but where each document differs substantially from the other. This pattern is very convenient for merging many legacy databases or sources of truth. Another common scenario combines similar things into one collection. For example, we combine auto, house, and personal loans or incorporate movies, tv shows, and webinars into one collection.

If the queries across many document types are not a primary concern or the grouping is unacceptable, one may want the objects in different collections. For querying many collections as one, look at the $union stage of the *Aggregation Framework* in the MongoDB documentation.

Details of the Inheritance Pattern

Traditional relational databases often model inheritance with one table containing the common part of the objects. Then each specialization is modeled with a separate table. Similarly, with source code, the common part would be the "super" class or the "parent" class. Subclasses inherit from the parent class and implement the specialization of each type.

The polymorphic nature of documents allows MongoDB to group the different objects in the same collection. Whether we decide to group the objects in the same collection depends on the answer to the following question: will we require to query across these documents? For example, a product catalog includes shirts, books, and shoes. If we want to query these products together, they should be in the same collection.

Querying across products means that the product types share more important fields than their differences. For different products, price, identifying product number, and desirability by shoppers on the site are sufficient reasons to justify putting the documents in the same collection.

One recommended document layout is to put common fields (price, product_id, etc.) in the document's root and isolate specificities in a subdocument. For example, a book may have a book subobject, while a shirt may have a shirt subobject. This way, passing the <object>.book subdocument to a section of the code that knows how to deal with this part makes the code cleaner. The calling code does not need to know what is inside the book subdocument.

Polymorphism may also appear in sections of the objects. For example, the book and the shirt have a size; however, the units or way to describe the size differs for both entities. Again, using a subobject to encapsulate the difference better organizes the information of the objects.

```
// a Product document for a book
{
    "_id": "10238845",
    "object_type": "book",
    "price": "49.99",
    "book": {
        "author": "Steve Hoberman",
        "publisher": "Technics Publications",
        ...
    }
    "size": {
        "width": "20 cm",
        "height": "30 cm",
        "depth": "2 cm"
    },
    ...
},
// a Product document for a shirt
{
    "_id": "10237777",
    "object_type": "shirt",
    "price": "49.99",
    "shirt": {
        "fabric": "cotton",
        ...
    }
    "size": {
        "code": "large"
    },
    ...
}
```

Figure 90 shows the schema for the above document.

Figure 90: Inheritance pattern schema example 1.

Implementing the Inheritance Pattern

To implement the *Inheritance Pattern,* take the following steps.

- Identify collections or entities that should live together.

- Identify common fields across these objects and place these fields in the root of the document.

- Identify fields varying by object type and place these under a subdocument.

- Add a field obj_type to keep track of the object type.

Example of applying the Inheritance Pattern with the pet adoption use case

In our Pet Adoption use case, we want to be able to query all birds, cats, and dogs to find information about their celebrity status, adoption information, etc. For this reason, the Pet collection implements the *Inheritance Pattern*. It contains different but similar objects: Birds, Cats, and Dogs. Furthermore, we added a pet_type field and grouped the specific fields of each pet type into a subobject.

If we did not use the pattern, we would have three collections respectively for the birds, cats, and dogs objects.

Here is an example of documents for each pet type.

```
// a Pet document for a bird
{
    "_id": "bird102345",
    "pet_type": "bird",
    "pet_name": "Birdie",
    ...
    "bird": {
        "bird_exotic_indicator": false
    }
},
// a Pet document for a cat
{
    "_id": "cat108545",
    "pet_type": "cat",
```

```
    "pet_name": "Tiger",
    ...
    "cat": {
        "cat_declawed_indicator": false
    }
},
// a Pet document for a dog
{
    "_id": "dog102345",
    "pet_type": "dog",
    "pet_name": "Rex",
    ...
    "dog": {
        "dog_good_with_children_indicator": true
    }
},
```

Figure 91 shows the schema for the above documents.

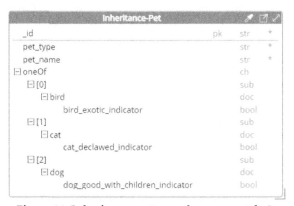

Figure 91: Inheritance pattern schema example 2.

Benefits of the Inheritance Pattern

The *Inheritance Pattern* is easy to implement. The foremost step is to group the objects we want to query together. Then optionally, we would create a subobject in these objects to isolate notable differences between things.

As there are ways to query together documents residing in different collections, the queries will be more straightforward if the documents live together. Additional benefits like using the *Atlas Search* functionality will also come from using a common collection.

There are ways to query many collections simultaneously with *Atlas Search*; however, it comes at the cost of complexity and possible limitations. So, it is preferred to query a single collection.

Trade-offs with the Inheritance Pattern

Indexing fields that only exist in some of the document types of a collection may be tricky. The designer must choose between regular indexes, sparse indexes, and partial indexes.

See the MongoDB documentation to learn more about the available indexes. Understanding MongoDB indexes is one essential knowledge you can acquire.

All these index types have their pros and cons. For example, a regular index would put an entry for all documents. If the field does not exist in the document, the value will be null, making it difficult to differentiate between an effective *null* value or the absence of the field.

Summary of the Inheritance Pattern

The *Inheritance Pattern* uses the fundamental aspect of polymorphism of the document model. The pattern allows keeping documents that differ a lot but share characteristics in a single collection. The most important read operations query the common fields of the documents.

Problem	<ul><li>Documents are more similar than different.</li><li>Need to query the documents on their similitudes.</li></ul>
Solution	<ul><li>Keep documents in a single collection.</li><li>Use a field to identify the document type.</li><li>Optionally, use a structure for commonalities and another for differences.</li></ul>
Use cases	<ul><li>Single View.</li><li>Product Catalog.</li><li>Content Management.</li></ul>
Benefits	<ul><li>Easy to implement.</li><li>Allow querying across a single collection.</li></ul>
Trade-offs	<ul><li>Secondary indexes may need the product type field. This field must appear in the queries to use the indexes.</li></ul>

Table 21: The Inheritance Pattern.

The Outlier Pattern

Should you make Justin Bieber the center of your attention?

Let's describe the context more with the following example. We want to design the next-generation social media messaging application that will overtake Twitter. Should we use Justin Bieber[8] as a representative user for our system?

Suppose we hope to attract the 8.023 billion people on the planet[9] to use this new system. In that case, we should look at the characteristics of typical users of social media networks. Each typical user may have a few dozen followers compared to the tens of millions a pop singer would have.

The hugely popular artists would be called "outliers" in such systems. Outliers have characteristics that make them different from the rest. The problem with outliers is that they do not represent what is typical.

When considering outliers, they skew the overall population. Some metrics like a "mean" may not mean

---

[8] The reference to this artist may be an indicator of this publication's age.

[9] Here is another hint of this publication's age.

much. This variance may not always be an issue, or the skewing effect may be small enough that it is inconsequential.

However, when dealing with big data, the differences between the outliers and what is "normal" can be huge, not just in terms of numbers but in terms of the implications they can have on the design of an application.

Overall description of the Outlier Pattern

The *Outlier Pattern* handles situations where a small percentage of documents or relationships would lead to a sub-optimal solution. By applying this pattern, the solution performs well in most cases (let's say 99%).

Applications modeling social networks or other applications having unusual actors in their systems can benefit from utilizing this pattern.

If the increased complexity in code is unacceptable, consider using the *Bucket Pattern* instead.

Details of the Outlier Pattern

The *Outlier Pattern* is not specific to MongoDB. Any other database can profit from it. However, the need for this sort of optimization often surfaces with big data applications. It is easier to apply with modern databases.

The essence of the pattern is to find the optimal solution for the problem as if the outliers did not exist. Then we define a different solution for the outliers.

For example, going back to our example of the social network application, we may embed an array of extended references to the followers of a given user, up to 1000 followers. Any user with over 1000 followers will have a field to identify it as an outlier. A parameter such as "has_more_followers": true would work. Upon retrieving a user document, the code would see this field and issue a second query to get more followers. The list of the overflow of followers can be in another collection. We often use the *Bucket Pattern* in conjunction to model the additional followers in chunks.

Running a second query occasionally will produce better performance than running two queries for each user. We need to validate this hypothesis with the application's workload. If the outliers drive many more queries, the assumption that the second query is more profitable may not be correct, or the savings may be so tiny that it is not worth adding the complexity of a second query.

Running a second query is simple and clean in the code; however, performing a single query across all the documents may create complications. For example, an aggregation query, producing some roll-ups, is more challenging to write, especially for a human trying to build an ad-hoc query. Again, before implementing this pattern, we need to evaluate the impact of the outliers on the analysis.

Implementing the Outlier Pattern

To implement the *Outlier Pattern*, take the following steps:

- Identify a threshold for declaring some documents as outliers. A good rule is 1% of the documents or 1% of the workload.

- Add a field called `is_outlier` to the document root of all documents.

- Use additional documents or the *Bucket Pattern* to store the additional information spilling out of the primary document.

- Identify the location for the additional information, either the same or an additional collection.

- Modify the code to query and handle the outliers differently.

Example of applying the Outlier Pattern with the pet adoption use case

One of our application's requirements is to keep the interactions with a pet in an array. We keep the last seven days of these interactions directly in the Pet collection. This design works well to track the interactions for most of our pets but not for our celebrity pets, which may record thousands of interactions in the last week. If we decide to move the interactions to a different collection and use many documents, we will pay the price of a join for each pet we look at. So, instead of modeling for these extreme cases, we decide to go on with the initial model and create an overflow collection for our pets that have had more than 100 interactions in the last seven days. The documents in the `pet` and `additional_interaction` collections would look like the following.

```
// a Pet document with a typical number
// of interactions
{
    "_id": "dog19370824",
    "name": "Fanny",
    "interactions": [
        {
            "ts": ISODate("2023-02-14T22:14:00Z"),
            "userid": 34717
        },
        {
            "ts": ISODate("2023-02-15T20:00:00Z"),
            "userid": 31043
        }
    ]
}
```

Figure 92 shows the schema for the above document.

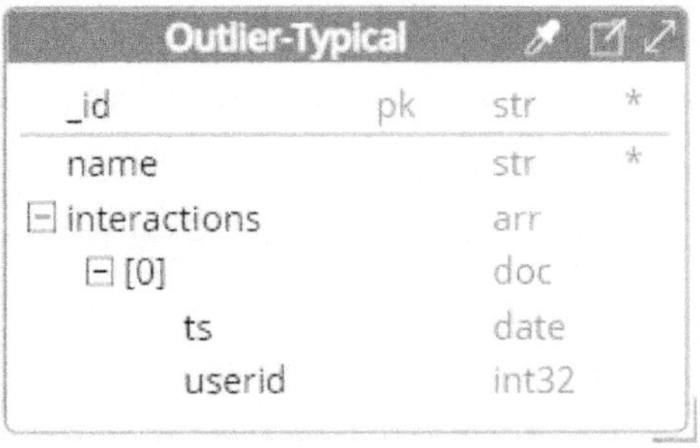

Outlier-Typical			
_id	pk	str	*
name		str	*
⊟ interactions		arr	
⊟ [0]		doc	
ts		date	
userid		int32	

Figure 92: Outlier pattern schema example 1.

```
// a Pet document with a typical number
// of interactions
// modeled as an outlier
{
    "_id": "bird102345",
    "name": "Lady G",
    "has_more_interactions": true,
    "interactions": [
        {
            "ts": ISODate("2023-02-01T20:14:00Z"),
            "userid": 34718
        },
        {
            "ts": ISODate("2023-02-01T20:00:00Z"),
            "userid": 31843
        }
        ...
    ]
}
```

Figure 93 shows the schema for the above document.

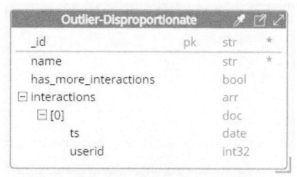

Figure 93: Outlier pattern schema example 2.

```
// additional_interactions documents for Lady G
{
    "_id": ObjectId('6358d092eb317a6b52baf752'),
    "pet_id": "bird102345",
    "name": "Lady G",
    "interactions_sequence": 1,
    "interactions": [
        {
         "ts": ISODate("2023-02-01T21:15:00Z"),
         "userid": 34718
        },
        {
         "ts": ISODate("2023-02-01T21:02:00Z"),
         "userid": 31893
        }
        ...
    ]
},
{
    "_id": ObjectId('6358d092eb317a6b52baf758'),
    "pet_id": "bird102345",
    "name": "Lady G",
    "interactions_sequence": 2,
    "interactions": [
        {
         "ts": ISODate("2023-02-01T22:15:00Z"),
         "userid": 34768
        },
```

```
    {
     "ts": ISODate("2023-02-01T22:02:00Z"),
     "userid": 34593
    }
    ...
  ]
}
```

Figure 94 shows the schema for the above document.

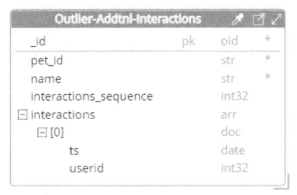

Figure 94: Outlier pattern schema example 3.

The following query would extract all interactions as single documents and report the count for a given pet.

```
db.pet.aggregate([
  {
    $match:
      {
        _id: "bird102345",
      },
  },
  {
    $unionWith:
      {
        coll: "pattern_outlier_ext",
        pipeline: [
          {
```

```
            $match: {
                pet_id: "bird102345",
              },
            },
          ],
        },
      },
      {
        $unwind:
          {
            path: "$interactions",
          },
      },
      {
        $count:
          "nb_interactions",
      },
])
```

Benefits of the Outlier Pattern

The main benefit of the *Outlier Pattern* is to focus on the system's overall performance. Instead of leveraging from the bottom, it makes most queries run faster to the detriment of a few.

Trade-offs with the Outlier Pattern

The work to support this pattern is done in the application, rendering the code more complex. For example, upon detecting an outlier document, the application runs additional queries and groups the results. And obviously, this extra code needs to be added and maintained.

Ad-hoc queries that need to run on all documents, like analytic queries, will be more challenging to write. The same query in the code will also be more complex to run.

Summary of the Outlier Pattern

The *Outlier Pattern* treats a few documents differently to prevent their outstanding characteristics from skewing the model to a degraded (non-optimal) solution.

Problem	• A few documents would lead to a suboptimal solution.
Solution	• Implement a solution that models the majority of the documents optimally.
	• Identify the outlier documents with a field.
	• Handle the outlier documents differently in the application.
Use cases	• Social networks.
	• One-to-many or many-to-many relationships differ considerably between the median and P95 to P99.
Benefits	• Optimized solution for most use cases.
Trade-offs	• Must be handled in the application.
	• May add a fair amount of complexity to the code.
	• Added difficulty for ad-hoc or analytic queries.

Table 22: The Outlier Pattern.

The Preallocated Pattern

We wish all airlines and car rental companies would use this pattern in their designs. If each seat or car was an element in their application directly associated with a customer, then we could be sure someone who bought a ticket or made a reservation gets the exact thing they reserved. Unfortunately, too often, predictive models match demand and availability. Ultimately, you may get a car, just not the one you wanted.

Overall description of the Preallocated Pattern

The *Preallocated Pattern* allocates a section of the document, mostly an array, to receive future data. Applications with a fixed set of objects like tickets, seats, and rooms can benefit from this pattern. Similarly, one can represent the time availability of a resource by a fixed number of slots and use this pattern to have one subobject per slot.

This pattern's relevance is usually associated with how database engines perform updates. For systems with high parallelism, one may prefer using one document per object or the *Bucket Pattern* to avoid concurrency issues.

Applications using a recent version of MongoDB use this pattern less frequently. In the early days of MongoDB, the MMAP storage engine often required this pattern to perform well. Any object subject to a fair amount of growth may have used the pattern.

Details of the Preallocated Pattern

In the early days of MongoDB, the storage engine mapped files in memory. Trying to read a document on a page that was not in memory would have the operating system bring the page in. It was a cheap and quick way to have a storage engine for the database.

A document could only extend to the free space up to the following adjacent document when it grew. More growth than that would require pushing all documents in the file. This reallocation of space was expensive, so the solution was to move the document to a larger hole or at the end of the file. Moving a document posed a problem because its references had to be updated. So, one of the popular patterns was to preallocate a larger document to accommodate its growth.

This concept of reserving space is similar to traditional relational databases, where we define the size of strings with the schema. We can grow fields, documents, and objects by allocating more space than needed during the design.

Another use case for the *Preallocated Pattern* is initializing arrays, cells, and maps. The code in the application may be easier to write and understand if the expected element exists and have a null value instead of testing for the existence of the element. For example, if we are to store a daily value for a metric in a document, it may be easier to allocate an array with 31 (or 28, 29, 30) elements. In this situation, space is well-spent because it will all be used by the end of the month.

Implementing the Preallocated Pattern

Take these steps to implement the *Preallocated Pattern*:

- Estimate the final size of the object.

- Decide if one or a sum of documents should model the object.

- Create an array field with the final dimension.

- Or create empty fields as placeholders.

- When the storage engine works with in-place updates, place a dummy value in each cell so the updates will not grow the document.

Example of applying the Preallocated Pattern with the pet adoption use case

Another of the requirements of our Pet Adoption application is to keep track of which pet is in which room or cage presently and in the planned future. Two possible solutions are:

- Have one document per room for many days.
- Have one document for all rooms per day.

With either solution, we could use the *Preallocated Pattern*. Pets being adopted, not behaving, or needing new playmates are all good reasons to move our pets around. Therefore let's take the second solution, which works better when considering that pets will be swapping locations often, and knowing their exact location is necessary for a few days at a time.

Our solution will create an array for the total number of habitations and spots available in the facility.

```
// a Room document with some pets assigned to them
{
    "_id": "2023-03-03",
    "rooms": [
        { "no": "101", "capacity": 2, "current": 2,
          "pets": ["dog204856", "dog178333"] },
        { "no": "102", "capacity": 3, "current": 0,
          "pets": [] },
        { "no": "103", "capacity": 4, "current": 0,
          "pets": [] },
        . . .
    ]
}
```

Figure 95 shows the schema for the above document.

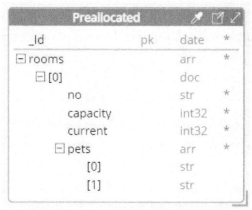

Figure 95: Preallocated pattern schema example.

There are a few things to notice in this design. First, the rooms without pets are still in the array. This characteristic is the essence of the *Preallocated Pattern*. We want to have all entries present for our application, where it will be easier to get zero-values or empty arrays instead of testing for the absence of entries.

The current field indicates data duplication of the number of pet array elements. It is easy to compute and keep up to date and will provide many optimizations versus calculating it all the time. This design is typical for systems where more read operations than write operations happen on this field (for the details on these pre-calculations, see the *Computed Pattern*).

Benefits of the Preallocated Pattern

A storage engine that allows physical in-place updates usually doesn't handle moving a document to another location very well. This pattern will prevent such a move by adequately initializing the document and permitting in-place updates.

With *WiredTiger*, MongoDB's current storage engine, there is no such thing as an in-place update. Updates operations create new versions of the documents.

Trade-offs with the Preallocated Pattern

The *Preallocated Pattern* would take a considerable amount of unnecessary space to prevent the documents from being moved. Therefore, in the case of documents that are likely to remain sparsely populated, for instance, an array of ten thousand elements with only one thousand cells in use, using a sparse array would be a better solution.

Summary of the Preallocated Pattern

The *Preallocated Pattern* can prevent a document from growing in size. The pattern usefulness profoundly depends on the storage engine[10] internals.

---

[10] The old storage engine (MMAP) in MongoDB 4.0 and earlier is doing in-place updates. The newer storage engine (WiredTiger) rewrites documents for each update, lessening the usefulness of this pattern.

Problem	• Constantly growing arrays may lead to bad performance with some database storage engines.
Solution	• Create an empty array with a constant dimension and optionally empty values to prevent the document from growing.
Use cases	• Assigning seat maps. • Scheduling rooms.
Benefits	• Prevents documents from being moved to a new location for storage engine using physical in-place updates.
Trade-offs	• Creates larger documents.

Table 23: The Preallocated Pattern.

The Schema Versioning Pattern

Do you have "Alter Table" nightmares? Memories of modifying the schema of your relational database or performing complex tasks under pressure to limit the amount of downtime for your users?

You will love the pattern we will cover in this section. It makes modifying the schema used by your application a much smoother process.

When an application uses a database, the question is not "If you will update your schema?", but "When would you update the schema?" Nearly all applications, in their lifetime, will require updates to the database schema.

Unfortunately, those updates take time and require downtime for Relational Databases. If anything goes wrong when we re-open the service, it may be challenging to revert to what we had before the migration.

Overall description of the Schema Versioning Pattern

The *Schema Versioning Pattern* sets the framework in the documents so schema migration can happen seamlessly. The pattern is straightforward. The work occurs in the application managing many document versions. The reward is no downtime for nearly any schema change.

All applications requiring a no-downtime operation can benefit from this pattern.

If downtime is acceptable for the application, someone may use the traditional way of migrating a schema and the data.

Details of the Schema Versioning Pattern

In a traditional relational database, there is one value for the schema version at a given time. We may extend the concept to one schema value per table if the tables are independent. Document databases can go deeper in versioning schemas. Because documents are polymorphic by nature, documents with different shapes can exist at a given time in a collection. A schema exists per document. In other words, each document can have its own schema version. This feature is an advantage for the document model. A migration goes from one version to another, so we need to lock or bring down the traditional relational database when we change the schema. From the perspective of the document database, we can migrate one document at a time, incurring no downtime. The migration can take minutes or days. Either way, we can perform the migration without downtime.

The *Schema Versioning Pattern* only requires keeping a schema version number per document. The first version of the document could omit the schema version number, as the absence would mean `schema_version: 1`.

The rest of the work relates to the application and the maintenance operations to perform the migrations.

On the application side, we need to add the code to support both versions, the current one and the upcoming one. We divide the code changes into handling documents of different shapes to display or process the data and having queries that can still work for a set of documents regardless of whether the documents have the same shape. Queries will be more complicated, and one may decide only to have a limited number of queries work for the period the documents are being migrated.

The migration operation starts by deploying the update application that works with both document shapes. Then documents can be migrated in the background through a script or migrated upon an update to the document[11]. This latter strategy of not migrating all documents requires keeping the code that handles each version in the application until all documents of a given version are updated. We prefer the first strategy of migrating all documents. However, we have seen users with many billion documents choosing the second strategy.

In the end, the keyword is *strategy*. We are in the driver's seat to decide how the migration will happen, if downtime is acceptable, etc.

---

[11] A few customers with large databases chose the strategy of only updating documents that are still relevant. Such documents are migrated as they receive an update.

Implementing the Schema Versioning Pattern

To implement the *Schema Versioning Pattern*, take the following steps:

- Add a schema_version field to the document of the collection to migrate.

- Add the code in the application to handle the documents' current shape and future shape.

- Increment the version number in `schema_version` when we go through the migration.

Example of applying the Schema Versioning Pattern with the pet adoption use case

As mentioned earlier, applying the pattern is very easy. The difficulty and work are in the operations and additional temporary code to perform the migrations.

Imagine we want to deploy Atlas Search on our project, or any Lucene-based search functionality, to search for pet names or breeds across traits, comments, and descriptions. To accomplish this requirement and make the maintenance easy on the search index, we want to group most of the criteria subject to search in a subdocument. We are saying "most of" because some may stay at the document's root. We want new fields that are dropped into the subdocument to get automatically indexed in the search. The current document may look like the following. All fields appear at the root of the document. Note also that we may not have planned to apply the *Schema Versioning Pattern*, so `schema_version` may not exist in the documents, which we will correlate to the value being 1.

```
// a Pet document with a schema version before
// migration
{
    "_id": "bird102345",
    "schema_version": 1,
    "pet_name": "Lady G",
    "breeds": [ "Nightingale" ],
    "breed_main_traits":
        [ "Found mostly in Europe",
          "European Robin",
          "Best singing bird" ],
    "colors": [ "brown", "white" ]
}
```

Figure 96 shows the schema for the above document.

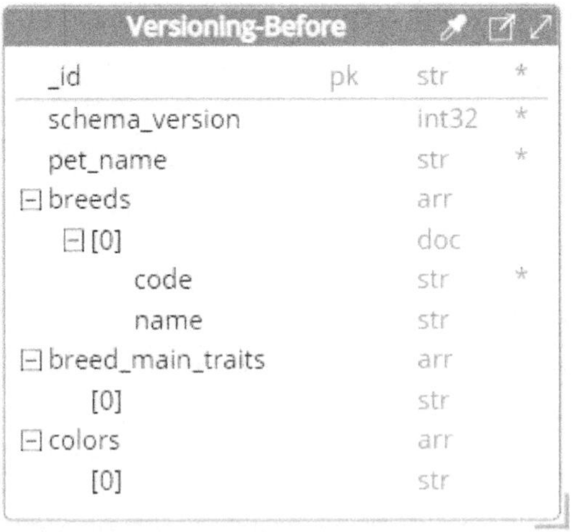

Figure 96: Schema versioning pattern example 1.

Then, we create a subdocument called "searchable_attributes" and move the attributes we want to enable our text search on in this new subdocument.

```
// a Pet document with a schema version after
// migration
{
    "_id": "bird102345",
    "schema_version": 2,
    "pet_name": "Lady G", // Part of the search index
    "searchable_attributes": {
        "breeds": [ "Nightingale" ],
        "breed_main_traits":
            [ "Found mostly in Europe",
              "European Robin",
              "Best singing bird"]
    }
}
```

Figure 97 shows the schema for the above document.

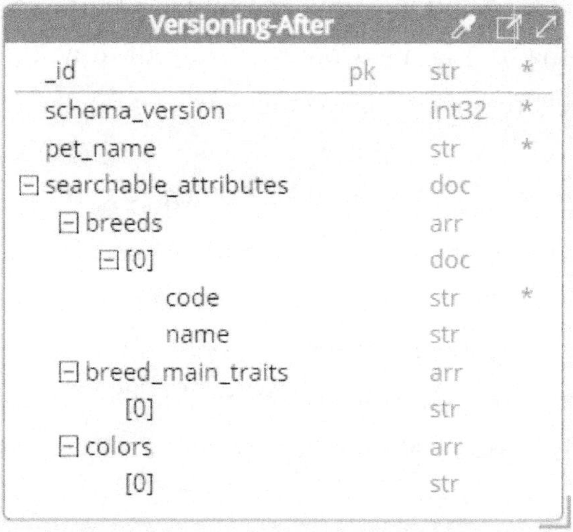

Versioning-After			
_id	pk	str	*
schema_version		int32	*
pet_name		str	*
⊟ searchable_attributes		doc	
⊟ breeds		arr	
⊟ [0]		doc	
code		str	*
name		str	
⊟ breed_main_traits		arr	
[0]		str	
⊟ colors		arr	
[0]		str	

Figure 97: Schema versioning pattern example 2.

With a search index on ["pet_name", "searchable_attributes"], our collection is ready for Atlas Search with the ability to add searchable attributes without updating the index.

The application's code needs to handle the two versions of documents by processing them correctly until we complete the migration. Then we can remove the code that handles version 1 of our schema.

Benefits of the Schema Versioning Pattern

As mentioned earlier, applying the pattern is very easy. The difficulty and work are in the operations and additional temporary code to perform the migrations.

This pattern is one of the most underrated abilities of MongoDB. Applying this pattern and the associated operations to migrate a schema without downtime is one of the best reasons to use MongoDB.

Trade-offs with the Schema Versioning Pattern

To avoid downtime, we must add the code to handle the new version before we remove the code that handles the current version. For some queries that aggregate all documents, it may translate to running two queries, one for each version of the documents, and combining the results.

Summary of the Schema Versioning Pattern

Problem	• Doing a schema migration without downtime.
Solution	• Add a schema version number to each document. • Modify the application code to handle each schema variant. • Progressively update each document.
Use cases	• Any application that can't sustain any downtimes.
Benefits	• Allow for schema migration without downtime.
Trade-offs	• Adds temporary complexity to the code to handle different schema variants.

Table 24: The Schema Versioning Pattern.

The Single Collection Pattern

This pattern helped Amazon migrate many applications from traditional relational databases.[12] The applications going to NoSQL databases often used this pattern to match tight performance and cost requirements.

Overall description of the Single Collection Pattern

The *Single Collection Pattern* is an adaptation of the *Single Table Pattern*[13] for the Document Model. The *Single Collection Pattern,* which is sometimes called the *Adjacency Pattern,* groups related documents of different types into a single collection. The documents would have otherwise been in various collections. Three characteristics define the pattern.

- Having all related documents in the same collection.

- Having relationships between the documents in one field or array of the given document.

---

[12] Rick Houlihan ran the team helping all the other groups migrate their application. You can see many of his presentations on the *Single Collection Pattern* on the Web.

[13] The *Single Table Pattern* is used extensively with Amazon's DynamoDB.

- Having an index on the field or array that maps the relationships and supports retrieving all related documents in a single query with a simple index scan.

Applications with high-velocity queries or many-to-many relationships where it is preferable to avoid data duplication can benefit from the *Single Collection Pattern*. A catalog of product items with many relationships to other products or components is an ideal case for this pattern. Similarly, an insurance company could group users, profiles, policies, claims, and messages in a single collection to quickly access a given set of objects.

If data duplication is acceptable for a set of fields in the many-to-many relationships, one may use the Extended Reference Pattern.

The Single Collection Pattern has the following variants:

- Using an array of references.
- Overloading a field.

Details of the Single Collection Pattern

Let's take the example of a shopping cart, where there is a cart with several items.

Variant A - Using an array of references

The first thing to do is add the field `docType` to the documents. Adding this field will allow a query to target documents as if they were in their original collection.

The second thing to do is model the relationships by adding an array of references `relatedTo` between the documents. The `relatedTo` entries model the connections between objects. In this case, a `cart` document will point to itself and all the items in the cart. From the other side of the relationship, the `item` documents point to the `cart` in which they are.

The magic happens when putting all the references in an array and indexing the array. The significant performance boost results from running a single query, minimizing the overhead of opening many connections and running many queries.

The following query will retrieve all items and the cart at once.

```
db.shopping_docs.find({"relatedTo": "20221206114523-
125489"})
```

A query to retrieve only the cart's items will use the `docType` and look like the following:

```
db.shopping_docs.find({"relatedTo": "20221206114523-
125489", "docType": "item"})
```

Variant B - Overloading a field

Alternatively, to model the relationships as an array of references, one can model the relationships by overloading the value of a field, often the _id field, in all documents. For example, the _id may have the following shape for the different documents in the single collection:

```
// Cart,    example: "20221206114523-125489"
_id: "<cartId>"


// Item     example: "20221206114523-125489/1"
_id: "<cartId>/<itemId>"
```

Now, we can find a cart with the following query.

```
db.shipping_docs.find({"_id": "20221206114523-
125489"})
```

Or find the cart and all items in it with a regular expression. The regular expression matches all documents that start with the cartId.

```
db.shipping_docs.find({"_id": /^20221206114523-
125489/})
```

Or find only the items in the cart by querying the documents with the cartId and a slash character. The query is filtering out the cart document.

```
db.shipping_docs.find({"_id": /^20221206114523-
125489\//})
```

or

```
db.shipping_docs.find({"_id": /20221206114523-
125489/, "docType": "item"})
```

Using the `_id` field to model the relationship requires limiting the relationships to one-to-many (no many-to-many relationships). Or in other words, the organization of the hierarchy is a tree, not a graph.

There is no `relatedTo` array, only the `_id` field. The `_id` field is always indexed. We use the field carrying the overload to find related documents.

One benefit of this variant is that the parent document doesn't need to be updated when we add a child. In the variant using an array of references, pointing to the new child requires modifying the parent. In other words, relationships are unidirectional.

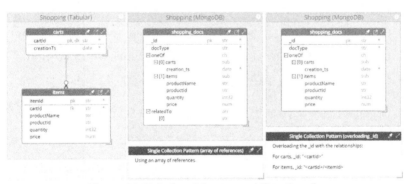

Figure 98: Relationships are unidirectional.

Implementing the Single Collection Pattern

To implement the *Single Collection_Pattern*, take the following steps.

- Elect to use an array of related documents or overload the _id field to represent the relationships.

- Add a docType to the documents.

- Place the documents of the various collections into one collection.

Example of applying the Single Collection Pattern with the pet adoption use case

Our Pet Adoption application needs to enable customers to purchase pet celebrity merchandise through our online store. Think of Amazon, but with everything related to pet accessories or swag depicting our pet celebrities. The relationships between the different entities we are placing in the single collection order_data are:

- A customer has one-to-many orders
- Each order has one-to-many shipments
- Each shipment has one-to-many items

Because we don't have many-to-many relationships, we have the choice of using the two variants described earlier. We select the variant overloading a field. The documents for an order would look like the following.

```
// a customer document
{
    "_id": "C#1",
    "doc_type": "customer",
    "customer_id": 1,
```

```
    "email": "steve_king@thriller.com"
},
// an order document
{
    "_id": "C#1#O#1",
    "doc_type": "order",
    "customer_id": 1,
    "order_id": 1,
    "date": "2023-03-03 13:13:13",
    "address": "1 University, Palo Alto,
California, USA"
},
// first shipment
{
    "_id": "C#1#O#1#S#1",
    "doc_type": "shipment",
    "customer_id": 1,
    "order_id": 1,
    "shipment": 1,
    "date": "2023-03-04 14:14:14"
},
// second shipment
{
    "_id": "C#1#O#1#S#2",
    "doc_type": "shipment",
    "customer_id": 1,
    "order_id": 1,
    "shipment": 2,
    "date": "2023-03-05 15:15:15"
},
// first item, part of the first shipment
{
    "_id": "C#1#O#1#S#1#I#1",
    "doc_type": "item",
    "customer_id": 1,
    "order_id": 1,
    "shipment": 1,
    "item": 1,
    "product": "Gourmet cat food"
},
// second item, part of the first shipment
```

```
{
    "_id": "C#1#O#1#S#1#I#2",
    "doc_type": "item",
    "customer_id": 1,
    "order_id": 1,
    "shipment": 1,
    "item": 2,
    "product": "Litter box"
},
// third item, part of the second shipment
{
    "_id": "C#1#O#1#S#2#I#3",
    "doc_type": "item",
    "customer_id": 1,
    "order_id": 1,
    "shipment": 2,
    "item": 3,
    "product": "Litter bag - 10 kg"`
}
```

Figure 99 shows the schema for the above documents.

We can find all the documents related to this order by simply querying the index with the following query.

```
db.order_data.find({"_id": /^C#1#O#1/})
```

Figure 99: Single collection pet schema.

Benefits of the Single Collection Pattern

The main benefit of this pattern is the performance improvement it provides versus joining documents. High-velocity queries and low-latency requirements benefit most from this pattern.

Because documents can be broken into smaller documents and still perform well, it is a good candidate pattern to use for many-to-many relationships.

Trade-offs with the Single Collection Pattern

Collections using this pattern look different due to the overloaded _id or the relatedTo array. Some indexes may have to be substituted with partial indexes to filter out the other types of documents not concerned by the queries and the queries need to include the object type as the first field.

Instead of simply mapping a class to a collection, one has to filter the documents each class manages.

Summary of the Single Collection Pattern

The *Single Collection Pattern* is excellent for high-velocity queries or low-latency requirements. It is also a great pattern to avoid data duplication with many-to-many relationships. However, one should prefer embedding or the *Extended Reference Pattern* for the other scenarios where the solution prefers simplicity over performance.

Problem	• Important queries have a low-latency requirement and must pull information from many entities.
Solution	• Put the entities in a common collection.
	• Establish the relationships between the entities in a relatedTo field in each document.
	• Index the relatedTo field.
Use cases	• Products.
	• Many-to-many relationships.

Benefits	• Works well for very high-velocity queries.
	• Works well for queries with low latency requirements.
	• Allows for a single query to retrieve a set of documents requiring many queries or join operations.
	• Works well to model many-to-many relationships where embedding is not a good solution.
Trade-offs	• Adds complexity to the documents, indexes, and queries.
	• Adds complexity to the one-to-one mapping between application objects and database documents.

Table 25: The Single Collection Pattern.

The Subset Pattern

Friends, I can't go out and have a drink with you tonight. I pulled the product page of a beer kit I want to buy, and there are thirty-six thousand reviews to read.

It would take more time to read the reviews than to make the beer, let it ferment, bottle it, and drink it.

Seriously, a website would put some of the reviews on the product's main page. However, they are likely to put a dozen or so. An optimized system should be able to grab all the information about the product in one query.

Overall description of the Subset Pattern

The *Subset Pattern* extracts a section of information from one or many documents to put it in related documents.

Applications with many large documents where we want to utilize only a small section of the whole can benefit from this pattern. For example, one could use this pattern to model a product with its most recent reviews, a bank account with its last transactions, a device with its latest measurements, or a customer account with its latest interactions.

If data duplication is impossible or undesired, consider the *Single Collection Pattern*.

The *Subset Pattern* has the following variants:

- Splitting a one-to-many relationship.
- Splitting a document.

Details of the Subset Pattern

The common cases of the subset patterns are the following:

- Separating information from a large document into a set of documents and having a one-to-one relationship between the set of documents.
- Limiting an array to a subset of elements.

The main reason behind utilizing this pattern is the conflict we may encounter from the following three rules in the current design:

- Keep together information that we use together.
- Read only the information that we need.
- Avoid joins.

Variant A - Splitting a One-to-Many Relationship

To illustrate the use of this variant, let's use our e-commerce example. We represent each product as a document. We embed all reviews for a given product into the product document. The problem with this design is that if we get a lot of reviews, the document is large. And it potentially breaks the rule of "Read only the information that we need" because most users will not read all the reviews.

An alternative is to keep each review in a different document and assemble the product information with the reviews. But then, we are breaking the rule about avoiding joins.

Thinking more about the issue, we observe that most customers may be interested in reading only some reviews, so there is little need to fetch all the reviews all the time. The right solution is a middle ground between embedding everything or referencing everything. Generally, reasonable solutions to problems are often just in-between solutions instead of an extreme position.

With this insight, we can develop our answer. We will bring a small number of reviews into the product document. This number may be 5, 10, 20, or more, whatever satisfies most users. As for which reviews, we could use the latest or the most popular. Again it depends on what we think is appropriate for our application.

Variant B - Splitting a Document

Another situation where we violate the rule of "Read only the information that we need" is with large documents, from which we only use a fraction of the documents' fields. For example, imagine we have a complex product requiring tons of fields. If we look deeply into this document, we may see a group of fields that are never displayed on the main web page but are only helpful when a user wants more information about the product. A large document will take more time to read from the disk and occupy more space in RAM. If we have millions of these documents, then the amount of space taken by fields rarely consulted is magnified.

Similarly to reducing a document's size by offloading arrays, we could divide a document into two parts and establish a one-to-one relationship between the two documents. One document has the most used fields, while the other has the less used ones.

In practice, we use the "splitting a one-to-many relationship" variant more because a document tends to become large because of substantially growing arrays.

Implementing the Subset Pattern

To implement the *Subset Pattern*, take the following steps:

- Identify the array, the one-to-many relationship, or the set of fields to divide.

- In the case of an array, create a second collection to keep all the documents of the original array.

- Identify the rule to select documents to place in the main document.

- Create a script to refresh the documents from the collection with all documents to the main documents.

- Schedule the script or rely on a trigger to update the subset.

Example of applying the Subset Pattern with the pet adoption use case

To illustrate the Subset Pattern, remember that one of our requirements for our Pet Adoption application was to let interested customers see a few comments regarding the pet's breed on its main page.

Again, to avoid doing a costly join to the comments for that breed, we bring the top three comments for the breed into each pet's document.

Documents in the `breed_comments` collection may look like the following:

```
// breed comment documents
{
    "_id": ObjectId('6358d092eb317a6b52ba4758'),
    "breed_id": "breed101",
    "breed_name": "Dalmatian",
    "comment_rank": 1,
    "comment":
        "I owned ten Dalmatians over the years  \
        and this breed is the most loyal breed \
        I have ever encountered.               \
        Nevertheless, these dogs don't see     \
        themselves as dogs but as members of   \
        the family, with the same rights."
},
{
    "_id": ObjectId('6358d092eb317a6b52ba5758'),
    "breed_id": "breed101",
    "breed_name": "Dalmatian",
```

```
    "comment_rank": 2,
    "comment":
        "The one thing to know about Dalmatians    \
         is that they are subject to many illnesses \
         like deafness and kidney stones. Don't     \
         expect them to live as long as other       \
         breeds."
},
{
    "_id": ObjectId('6358d092eb317b6b82ba5758'),
    "breed_id": "breed101",
    "breed_name": "Dalmatian",
    "comment_rank": 3,
    "comment":
        "This is a very stubborn breed of dog.     \
         Expect to spend time training them.        \
         If you are not ready for this commitment, \
         you should choose another breed."
},
...
```

Figure 100 shows the schema for the above documents.

Figure 100: Subset pattern breed schema.

Applying the *Subset Pattern*, we bring the top three rated comments into each pet document.

```
// a Pet document
{
    "_id": "dog19370824",
```

```
    "name": "Fanny",
    "breeds": [
        {
            "code": "breed101",
            "name": "Dalmatian",
            "top_comments": [
    "I owned ten Dalmatians over the years  \
     and this breed is the most loyal breed \
     I have ever encountered.               \
     Nevertheless, these dogs don't see     \
     themselves as dogs but as members of   \
     the family, with the same rights.",
    "The one thing to know about Dalmatians    \
     is that they are subject to many illnesses \
     like deafness and kidney stones. Don't     \
     expect them to live as long as other
     breeds.",
    "This is a very stubborn breed of dog.     \
     Expect to spend time training them.       \
     If you are not ready for this commitment, \
     you should choose another breed."
            ]
        }
    ],
}
```

Figure 101 shows the schema for the above documents.

As discussed earlier, the *Subset Pattern* introduced data duplication. In this case, there is little of an impact. The comments in this pet document don't have to be in sync all the time with the ones from the `breed_comment` collection. A periodic job can adjust the comments.

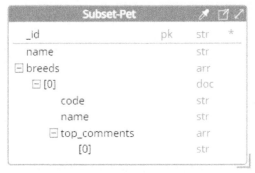

Figure 101: Subset pattern pet schema.

Benefits of the Subset Pattern

The main goal of this pattern is to reduce the size of the working set in memory, which it does by avoiding loading too much information at first. Because the document contains everything it needs, but no more it would load quickly, providing a low latency to systems that require it, like user-facing applications.

Trade-offs with the Subset Pattern

We need more round-trips to the server when offloading data from one document to another collection.

Often all the objects on the many-side will be present in the second collection, while we keep a subset with the main document. This situation creates data duplication for the copied objects in the main document. One may avoid this duplication by storing the documents in only one of the two locations; however, this would lead to more complex queries when aggregating all the documents.

Summary of the Subset Pattern

The *Subset Pattern* helps reduce the amount of RAM consumed by the system. We split the information between what needs to be accessed immediately and what can be accessed by a subsequent request.

Problem	• Large documents are taking up a lot of space in memory.
Solution	• Break up arrays of subdocuments to only keep a minimum number of elements all the time. • Migrate the remaining documents to a second collection.
Use cases	• List of reviews. • List of comments. • A long list of nearly anything kept in an array.
Benefits	• Smaller documents with shorter load time. • Smaller working set in memory.
Trade-offs	• More round-trips to the server. • Potentially creates data duplication.

Table 26: The Subset Pattern.

The Tree Pattern

Recently, the most incredible story happened to my cousin. He learned he had three blood brothers he did not know. Yes, we are talking about a family tree. However, family trees don't obey the definition of trees in computer science because each node has two parents, a father and a mother.

In computer science, a tree is a subcase of a graph. It is a graph without cycles, with each node having one and only one parent. Each node can have zero or many children. When a graph meets these criteria, we call it a tree.

Why is it important to understand if we are in the presence of a tree or a graph? The characteristics of a tree allow for some optimizations over a graph. First, a tree is easier to traverse, and there are no cycles to look for. In other words, it makes trees safe for recursive code.

The *Tree Pattern* shares common fields and operations with the *Graph Pattern*; however, it serves us well to use the correct pattern for the data structure.

Overall description of the Tree Pattern

We could use a graph database, but we may want to avoid adding a database system for the same reasons as with the *Graph Pattern*.

Applications with catalogs with a clear hierarchy of categories can profit from this pattern. Documents, including organizational hierarchies of people, divisions, regions, stores, or other, typically depicted with a tree diagram, are also good candidates for using this pattern.

The *Tree Pattern* has the following variants:

- Referencing the parent.
- Referencing the children.
- Referencing the ancestors.
- Using hybrid references.

Details of the Tree Pattern

As stated earlier, it is vital to understand that a tree structure is a subcase of a graph structure. It is a graph without cycles, with each node having only one parent.

Let's use the following tree of products for the examples in this section to illustrate the tree designs. The tree organizes the products by category. For example, "running shoes" are part of the "shoes" category, which in its turn is part of the "sportswear" category.

```
- Sportswear
  - Clothes
    - Jerseys
    - Shorts
  - Shoes
    - Running shoes
```

Variant A - Referencing the parent

This variant is the simplest model. In each document, a scalar field defines a reference to the parent document. The value of the `parent` is the identifier or primary key of the referenced document.

```
// reference to the parent
{
    "_id": "cat10001",
    "name": "Sportswear",
    "parent": "root"
}, {
    "_id": "cat11001",
    "name": "Clothes",
    "parent": "cat10001"
}, {
    "_id": "cat11101",
    "name": "Jerseys",
    "parent": "cat11001"
}, {
    "_id": "cat11102",
    "name": "Shorts",
    "parent": "cat11001"
}, {
    "_id": "cat12001",
    "name": "Shoes",
    "parent": "cat10001"
}, {
    "_id": "cat12101",
    "name": "Running shoes",
    "parent": "cat12001"
}
```

Figure 102 shows the schema for the above documents.

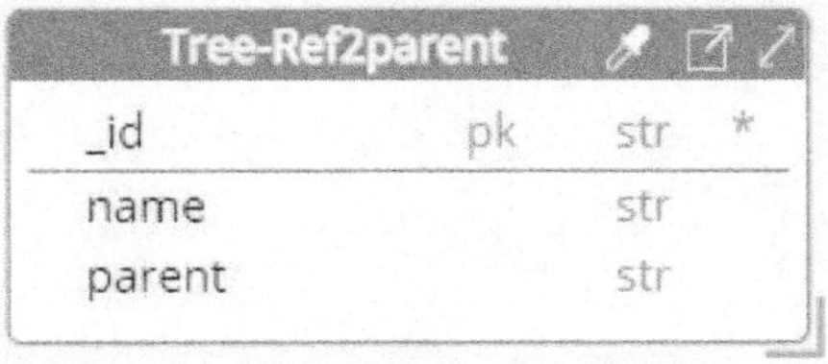

Figure 102: Tree pattern schema example 1.

An application walks the tree up by fetching the nodes individually. Alternatively, we can retrieve all ancestor nodes using an aggregation query with the $graphLookup stage.

This variant is the easiest one to update when the tree structure changes.

Variant B - Referencing the children

In this variant, we keep an array of references to the children. We need to use an array because we can have more than one child for a given node.

```
// references to the children
{
    "_id": "cat10001",
    "name": "Sportswear",
    "children": ["cat11001", "cat12001"]
}, {
    "_id": "cat11001",
    "name": "Clothes",
    "children": ["cat11101", "cat11102"]
}, {
    "_id": "cat11101",
    "name": "Jerseys",
    "children": []
}, {
    "_id": "cat11102",
    "name": "Shorts",
```

```
    "children": []
}, {
    "_id": "cat12001",
    "name": "Shoes",
    "children": ["cat12101"]
}, {
    "_id": "cat12101",
    "name": "Running shoes",
    "children": []
}
```

The schema for the above documents appears in Figure 103.

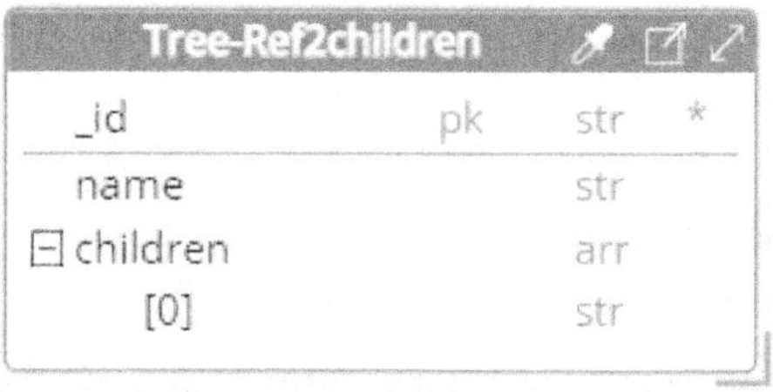

Figure 103: Tree pattern schema example 2.

An application walks the tree down by fetching the nodes individually. Alternatively, we can retrieve all ancestor nodes using an aggregation query with the $graphLookup stage.

This variant is also easy to update when a parent-child relation changes. Move the node to the children's array of its new parent node.

Variant C - Referencing the ancestors

We call this variant "referencing the ancestors." However, for convenience, we often also reference the direct parent. The main advantage of this variant is that we don't need to do recursive calls to go up the tree, as all the ancestors are already preidentified. As for the main disadvantage, well, it is that the ancestors are preidentified. Any change in a parent-child relation may impact many nodes for which we need to recalculate their `ancestors' array.

This variant departs from the *Graph Pattern* variants. It is only possible with a tree because the levels going up are limited to one. In other words, we don't have a variant using children.

```
// reference to the parent
{
    "_id": "cat10001",
    "name": "Sportswear",
    "parent": "root",
    "ancestors": ["root"]
}, {
    "_id": "cat11001",
    "name": "Clothes",
    "parent": "cat10001",
    "ancestors": ["root", "cat10001"]
}, {
    "_id": "cat11101",
    "name": "Jerseys",
    "parent": "cat11001",
    "ancestors": ["root", "cat10001", "cat11001"]
}, {
    "_id": "cat11102",
    "name": "Shorts",
    "parent": "cat11001",
    "ancestors": ["root", "cat10001", "cat11001"]
}, {
    "_id": "cat12001",
    "name": "Shoes",
    "parent": "cat10001",
    "ancestors": ["root", "cat10001"]
```

```
}, {
    "_id": "cat12101",
    "name": "Running shoes",
    "parent": "cat12001",
    "ancestors": ["root", "cat10001", "cat12001"]
}
```

Figure 104 shows the schema for the above documents.

Figure 104: Tree pattern schema example 3.

Variant D - Using hybrid references

Finally, the last variant uses a combination of the above. For example, the Shoes category may have all fields of variants A, B, and C.

```
// reference to the parent
{
    "_id": "cat12001",
    "name": "Shoes",
    "parent": "cat10001",
    "ancestors": ["root", "cat10001"],
    "children": ["cat12101"]
}
```

Figure 105 shows the schema for the above documents.

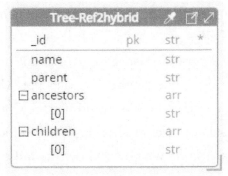

Figure 105: Tree pattern schema example 4.

This variant gives more options to retrieve the information quickly; however, the maintenance on this type of tree is higher if the parent-child relations change often. We should prefer this variant for optimizations and tree structures that are static, like mother-child relations.

Implementing the Tree Pattern

To implement the *Tree Pattern*, take the following steps.

- Identify which variant best balances performance and overhead for dealing with data duplication.

- Create a field containing references to either the parent, an array of references to the children, or the ancestors.

- Optionally, use a combination of references among the above.

- Create a script or a trigger to update the dependencies when needed.

Example of applying the Tree Pattern with the pet adoption use case

In our Pet Adoption use case, we want to track the information about the mother of each pet whenever the information is available. We would use the *Graph Pattern* if we kept track of the mother and the father. For this example, we assume we never know the father in this use case, so we cannot track it. We would therefore apply the *Tree Pattern* parent variant because a node (pet) only has one parent node.

```
// some Pet documents
// Fanny
{
    "_id": "dog19370824",
    "name": "Fanny",
    "sex": "female",
    "relatives": {
        "mother": "dog19350224"
    }
},
// Fanny's mother
{
    "_id": "dog19350224",
    "name": "Perdita",
    "sex": "female",
    "relatives": {
        // No info. She was a rescued dog.
    }
},
// Fanny's first child
{
    "_id": "dog20200110",
    "name": "Finn",
    "sex": "female",
    "relatives": {
```

```
        "mother": "dog19370824"
    }
},
// Fanny's second child
{
    "_id": "dog20201206",
    "name": "Canuck",
    "sex": "male",
    "relatives": {
        "mother": "dog19370824"
    }
}
```

Figure 106 shows the schema for the above documents.

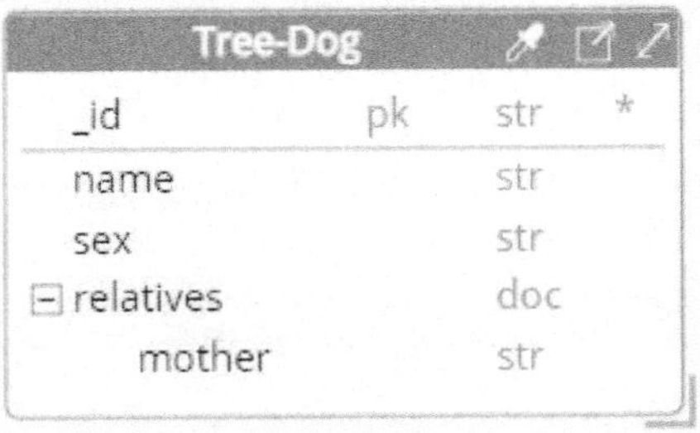

Figure 106: Tree pattern dog schema.

We can find Fanny's children by looking at the documents that have her as a mother.

```
db.pets.find({"relatives.mother":"dog19370824"})
```

Trying to find all the descendants of Fanny becomes a little more complicated. We can do it by adding a field to track the children or using an array to follow all the ancestors. Note that both alternatives create data duplication. However, these anomalies are maintenance-free as the parent-child, or ancestors' relationship does not change over time.

We can model the relationships using an array of children with the following.

```
// Fanny with an array of her children
{
    "_id": "dog19370824",
    "name": "Fanny",
    "relatives": {
        "mother": "dog19350224",
        "father": "dog19360824",
        "children": [ "dog20200110", "dog20201206"]
    }
}
```

Figure 107 shows the schema for the above documents.

Tree-Dog w/children			
_id	pk	str	*
name		str	
sex		str	
⊟ relatives		doc	
mother		str	
father		str	
⊟ children		arr	
[0]		str	

Figure 107: Tree pattern dog with children schema

Using the $graphLookup functionality of MongoDB, we can find all descendants of each pet with the following query.

```
db.pet.aggregate([
```

```
{
    "$graphLookup":
        {
            "from": "pet",
            "startWith": "$relatives.children",
            "connectFromField": "relatives.children",
            "connectToField": "_id",
            "as": "descendants",
            // limit the recursion in case we have wrong
            // circular links in the dataset
            "maxDepth": 10
        },
    },
])
```

Benefits of the Tree Pattern

The alternative of using only the parent variant of the *Tree Pattern* is simple and does not create data duplication or staleness. However, requests to parse many levels will be slower and require recursion.

The children variant is great for traversing a node and all its descendants. You can even use recursive code if you want.

The alternative of using the ancestors variant of the *Tree Pattern* gives excellent performance and may prevent any recursive calls. However, it creates data duplication.

Trade-offs with the Tree Pattern

As said above, some alternatives create data duplication when the edge between two nodes or ancestors exists in more than one document. It is not an issue if those relationships between nodes do not change. If they seldomly change, then the use of transactions permit to keep consistency at all time. In cases where the relationship changes often, only consider using the solution if staleness is acceptable for a given period of time. For example, shuffling products into categories where we frequently reorganize them is okay if a nightly job recalculates the ancestors, and we can tolerate the staleness of a daily update.

Summary of the Tree Pattern

The *Tree Pattern* allows modeling relationships between entities where each node has only one parent.

Problem	• Represent an organization of entities as a tree.
Solution	• Reference either or a combination of parents, child, and ancestor documents.
Use cases	• Organization charts. • Product categories.
Benefits	• Easy to maintain parent relationships. • Easy to navigate ancestor relationships.
Trade-offs	• Potentially creates data duplication.

Table 27: The Tree Pattern.

Additional resources: the MongoDB University free courses on data modeling.

Primary keys

Similarly to traditional relational databases, MongoDB has the concept of a primary key. This key is consistently named _id. The key can be a simple field or several fields. In the latter case, _id is a subobject in which all fields appear.

When the _id field is absent in the document to insert, MongoDB adds the field to the document. The value's type will be ObjectId, and the value is similar to UUID values. The primary key's values must be unique for the collection. MongoDB needs the unicity to replicate and track the document across the replicas.

```
// Example of default primary key inserted by MongoDB
{
    "_id": ObjectId("624c64e7102ffcabac4dabde"),
    "pet_name": "Lady G",
    ...
}
```

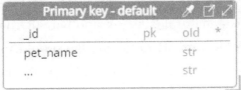

Figure 108: Primary key default.

```
// Example of a natural key used as the primary key
{
    "_id" : "bird102345",
    "pet_name": "Lady G",
    ...
}
```

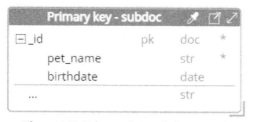

Figure 109: Primary key natural.

```
// Example of a subdocument used as the primary key
{
    "_id" : {
        "pet_name" : "Lady G",
        "birthdate" : ISODate("2021-02-01T00:00:00Z")
    },
    ...
}
```

Figure 110: Primary key subdocument.

If we have a natural key (or another alternate key) to identify the documents uniquely, we should use it as our Primary key. The reason is that _id already has a unique default index. This index saves the creation of an additional index while we underuse the default one.

If we fear possible duplicates, we prefer using an auto-generated ObjectId.

As for subdocuments, they bring some complications for indexes and searches. We recommend avoiding them. There are a few cases where subdocuments make sense. In the above example, uniqueness could not be determined only by the pet_name, so we added a birthdate. However, we are still constrained to have unique composite values for this pair of fields.

Schema validation

An important aspect, and often a limitation, of relational databases is that they operate on fixed, rigid schemas with a pre-determined structure of fields with known data types. MongoDB is much more flexible, as we've seen. But that does not mean that you should give up on data quality, consistency, or integrity.

Even in a flexible schema environment like MongoDB, where polymorphism is possible for different document types in a collection, validating documents being inserted or updated is a good practice. In essence, it allows you to achieve the best of both worlds: flexibility and quality.

MongoDB has a schema validation feature so you can apply constraints on the structure of your documents.

Schema validation is based[14] on JSON Schema (https://json-schema.org/), an open standard for JSON document structure description and validation.

In MongoDB, schema validation works by assigning a JSON Schema with your set of requirements to each collection where you want validation to occur. This is done using the $jsonSchema keyword within the "validator" option of a collection. If you decide to change the rules, you may replace the previous JSON Schema with a new one that represents your new validation requirements.

Constraints may include whether a field is required or not, the data type or types for a given field, min and/or max values for numbers and whether negative values are allowed, min and/or max length for strings, value enumerations, the max number of array items, the structure of subdocuments, etc. You may even define polymorphic structures allowed, and whether unknown fields can be added.

---

[14] The MongoDB implementation is a subset/superset of the JSON Schema draft-04 specification. It is extended to support MongoDB-specific features including additional data types. But it does not support all the features of the JSON Schema specification. See more at https://www.mongodb.com/docs/manual/reference/operator/query/jsonSchema/#omissions.

Depending on the validation level specified, the database engine will strictly refuse to insert a non-compliant document or have a tolerant behavior of inserting the document while returning a warning message to the application via the driver.

JSON Schema is a powerful standard, but it can be a bit complex at times. Hackolade Studio makes it simple by dynamically generating the syntactically correct $jsonSchema validator script without requiring any knowledge of JSON Schema.

This feature is not supposed to be a substitute for properly validating business rules in application code. But it provides additional safeguards to keep data meaningful beyond the shelf life of applications.

Monitoring schema evolution

Organizations operate in different ways. In many organizations following the principles in this book, data modeling happens in the initial stages of an Agile sprint or of an application change, then code changes occur and are implemented in the different environments.

In other organizations, development has the upper hand, and evolutions tend to happen in a code-first manner. In such cases, data modeling still can come in handy to help with data quality and consistency. We talk about "retroactive data modeling" or "data modeling after-the-fact."

This process is useful to identify inconsistencies, such as the presence of addresses using the field "zipcode" while others use "postalcode". It is critical also to identify potentially more damaging situations in the area of PII, GDPR, confidentiality, etc.

Hackolade Studio provides a Command-Line Interface to programmatically invoke many of the features available in the graphical user interface. It is easy to orchestrate a succession of commands. In a code-first approach, the structure in the database instance evolves first. Every night, a scheduled process goes through the following steps:

- Reverse-engineer the database instance.

- Compare the resulting model with the baseline model. This produces a "delta model" and optionally a "merged model".

- A manual step allows to review the model comparison and identify whether all changes in production are legitimate. Maybe adjustments are necessary to the code, or data needs migration.

- Commit the merged model, which becomes the new baseline model, resulting in publication to the corporate data dictionary so business users can be made aware of the evolution.

Schema migration

We have mentioned many times the great flexibility of the MongoDB document when it comes to easily modifying the schema as application requirements evolve. Compared to relational databases, achieving this with zero downtime, without the infamous migration weekends, or without blue/green deployments and other complex approaches is simple.

We have also highlighted the need to leverage the schema versioning pattern to help applications process the data with the appropriate business rules and enable backward compatibility.

Challenges quickly arise in large and complex environments, particularly when multiple applications read the same data. It is not efficient or practical to port convoluted business logic to multiple applications for dozens of schema evolutions over time. It even ends up burning useless CPU cycles to handle them. And should we mention the risks of misinterpretation and misguided business decisions due to a query unaware of some specific schema evolution?

New users of MongoDB discovering the flexibility of the document model often don't realize that it is a best practice in successful organizations to scrupulously perform schema migrations to reduce the technical debt of maintaining old schema versions in the data.

There are several schema migration strategies to consider. The choice of strategy will depend on the specific needs of the database and the business, and careful planning and testing are essential to ensure a successful migration. Some organizations are even known to have developed costing models to evaluate the tradeoffs of the different strategies.

Schema migration strategies can be broadly categorized into two basic approaches: eager migration and lazy migration. There are also hybrid strategies that combine aspects of both eager and lazy migration.

- Eager migration: schema changes are made all at once, and the data is migrated to the new schema immediately. Similar to what has been done with relational databases, this approach requires more planning and may result in downtime during the migration process, but it ensures that all data is immediately updated to the new schema.

- Lazy migration: schema changes are made incrementally, and the data is migrated to the new schema only when it is accessed or updated. This approach can be less disruptive and easier to implement, but it adds latency to common operations. Furthermore, it is possible that all the data might never be fully migrated to the new schema.

- Predictive migration: schema changes are made based on predictions of how the data will be used in the future. This approach requires more planning and analysis, but it can minimize the latency in common operations.

- Incremental migration: schema changes are made in small, iterative steps, and the data is migrated to the new schema progressively.

Both predictive and incremental migration can be offloaded to processes running in the background and/or during off-peak hours to minimize the impact on systems. You may also combine strategies depending on the remaining data to be migrated: start with a predictive migration while doing lazy migration opportunistically, then finish with incremental migration.

Step 3: Optimize

Similar to indexing, denormalizing, partitioning, and adding views to a RDBMS physical model, we would add database-specific features to the query refinement model to produce the query design model.

Indexing

MongoDB uses indexes to improve query performance by reducing the number of documents that need to be scanned to satisfy a query. MongoDB supports a variety of index types, including:

- default _id index: a unique index is created on the _id field during the creation of a collection. The _id index prevents clients from inserting two documents with the same value for the _id field. You cannot drop this index on the _id field.

- single field: MongoDB supports the creation of user-defined ascending/descending indexes on a single field of a document.

- compound index: user-defined indexes are also allowed on multiple fields, i.e. compound indexes.

- multikey index: multikey indexes are used to index the content stored in arrays. If you index a field that holds an array value, MongoDB creates separate index entries for every element of the array. These multikey indexes allow queries to select documents that contain arrays by matching on element or elements of the arrays. MongoDB automatically determines whether to create a multikey index if the indexed field contains an array value; you do not need to explicitly specify the multikey type.

- geospatial index: to support efficient queries of geospatial coordinate data, MongoDB provides two special indexes: "2d indexes" that use planar geometry when returning results and "2dsphere indexes" that use spherical geometry to return results.

- text index: a text index supports searching for string content in a collection. These text indexes do not store language-specific stop words (e.g. "the", "a", "or") and stem the words in a collection to only store root words.

- hashed indexes: to support hash-based sharding, MongoDB provides a hashed index type, which indexes the hash of the value of a field. These indexes have a more random distribution of values along their range, but only support equality matches and cannot support range-based queries.

Indexes can have the following properties:

- unique indexes: the unique property for an index causes MongoDB to reject duplicate values for the indexed field. Other than the unique constraint, unique indexes are functionally interchangeable with other MongoDB indexes.

- partial indexes: they only index the documents in a collection that meet a specified filter expression. By indexing a subset of the documents in a collection, partial indexes have lower storage requirements and reduced performance costs for index creation and maintenance. Partial indexes offer a superset of the functionality of sparse indexes and should be preferred over sparse indexes.

- sparse indexes: the sparse property of an index ensures that the index only contains entries for documents with the indexed field. The index skips documents that do not have the indexed field. The sparse index option can be combined with the unique index option to reject documents that have duplicate values for a field but ignore documents that do not have the indexed key.

- TTL indexes: time-to-live indexes are special indexes that MongoDB can use to automatically remove documents from a collection after a certain amount of time. This is ideal for certain types of information like machine-generated event data, logs, and session information that only need to persist in a database for a finite amount of time.

There are many reasons to use a data modeling tool to create and maintain indexing information, including better collaboration, documentation, ease of maintenance, and better governance. In addition to supporting all of the indexing options of MongoDB, Hackolade Studio also generates the index syntax so it can be applied to the database instance or given to an administrator to apply.

Sharding

Sharding is a method for distributing data across multiple machines. MongoDB uses sharding to support deployments with very large data sets and high throughput operations. Database systems with large data sets or high throughput applications can challenge the capacity of a single server. There are two methods for addressing system growth: vertical scaling (a bigger, more powerful server) and horizontal scaling (more servers with divided datasets). MongoDB supports horizontal scaling through sharding.

MongoDB partitions the collection using the shard key to distribute the documents in a collection. The shard key consists of an immutable field or fields that exist in every document in the target collection.

You choose the shard key when sharding a collection. The choice of a shard key can be changed after sharding, however, it is a costly operation. A sharded collection can have only one shard key.

MongoDB supports three sharding strategies for distributing data across sharded clusters: hashed sharding, ranged sharding, and tag-aware (or zoned):

- hashed sharding: it involves computing a hash of the shard key field's value. Each chunk is then assigned a range based on the hashed shard key values. MongoDB automatically computes the hashes when resolving queries using hashed indexes. Applications do not need to compute hashes.

- ranged sharding: it involves dividing data into ranges based on the shard key values. Each chunk is then assigned a range based on the shard key values.

- zone sharding (previously known as tag-aware): in sharded clusters, you can create zones representing a group of shards and associate one or more ranges of shard key values to that zone. MongoDB routes reads and writes that fall into a zone range only to those shards inside of the zone.

Just like for indexing, Hackolade Studio also generates the sharding syntax so it can be applied to the database instance or given to an administrator to apply.

Note that it used to be challenging to modify a shard key, once chosen. Starting with MongoDB version 5, it is now possible to "reshard" a collection.

In-Use encryption

MongoDB provides a field-level encryption ("FLE") framework, both server-side and client-side. Applications can encrypt fields in documents prior to transmitting data over the wire to the server. Only applications with access to the correct encryption keys can decrypt and read the protected data. Deleting an encryption key renders all data encrypted using that key as permanently unreadable.

Using Client-Side FLE alongside in-flight and at-rest encryption gives an end-to-end, complementary approach in building applications that provide a defense-in-depth security posture to address different threat models.

- In-flight encryption protects all data traversing the network, but does not encrypt data in-memory or at-rest.

- At-rest encryption protects all stored data, but does not encrypt data in-memory or in-flight.

- With client-side encryption, the most sensitive data never leaves applications in plain text. Fields that are encrypted client-side remain encrypted over the network, as they are being processed in database server memory, and at-rest in storage, backups, and logs.

Either server-side or client-side encryption can be used, or both. It is a good idea to have both server-side and client-side FLE because they complement each other. In the case of a legacy client, or a misconfigured client, server-side FLE eliminates the possibility that any plain text is used to insert or update a document, when it was meant to be encrypted. Conversely, a single person with access to the database does not have the power to disconnect field-level encryption if it is also implemented client-side.

Generation of test data

Manually generating fake data for testing and demos takes time and slows down the testing process, particularly if large volumes are required.

Using fake (a.k.a synthetic) data can be useful during system development, testing, and demos, mainly because it avoids using real identities, full names, real credit card numbers or Social Security Numbers, etc., while using "Lorem ipsum" strings and random numbers is not realistic enough to be meaningful.

Alternatively, one could use cloned production data, except that it generally does not exist for new applications, plus you would still have to mask or substitute sensitive data to avoid disclosing any personally identifiable information.

Synthetic data is also useful for exploring edge cases that lack real data or for identifying model bias.

With Hackolade Studio, you can generate first names and last names that look real but are not, and the same for company names, product names and descriptions, street addresses, phone numbers, credit card numbers, commit messages, IP addresses, UUIDs, image names, URLs, etc.

Data generated here may be fake, but it has the expected format and contains meaningful values. City and street names, for example, are randomly composed from elements that mimic real names. And you can set the desired locale so the data elements are localized for better contextual meaning.

Generating mock test data is a 2-step process:

- one-time setup for each model: you must associate each attribute with a function to get a contextually realistic sample

- each time you need to generate test data, you define the parameters of the run

Hackolade Studio generates the sample documents so they can be inserted in the database instance.

Three tips

1. **Workload analysis:** estimates of volume and velocity of access patterns have a major impact on your choice of schema design patterns. And it may evolve overtime, requiring to sometimes refactor the schema and corresponding application code. Fortunately, the JSON-like document model makes it much easier to evolve schema with MongoDB than for relational databases.

2. **Schema versioning:** it is not a matter of if your schema will evolve, but when. Changing customer needs, new strategic direction, unforeseen requirements, scope creep, continuous enhancements, iterative development, etc. It is a fact of life that your schema design will evolve over time. So you might as well organize yourself for that.

3. **Schema migration:** after baking cookies, one generally cleans the dishes and puts away the utensils. Don't forget to migrate your documents to the new schema version to eliminate the technical debt of schema evolution.

Three takeaways

1. **Data modeling is even more important for MongoDB than for relational databases:** JSON's flexibility and ease of evolution provide a false sense of security, as there are no guardrails like the rules normalization in relational databases. The consequence is that the responsibility to ensure consistency, integrity, and quality shifts elsewhere. The section earlier in the book on Schema Design Patterns illustrates the number of different ways one can design a schema. You must choose wisely the appropriate pattern(s) based on information gathered in the Align and Refine phases.

2. **Gather knowledge and experience from different stakeholders and domain experts:** developers might be tempted to design schemas all by themselves. There's no doubt that they possess the technical knowledge to design a schema for a JSON document. But to avoid rework of the application code, it is more efficient to first understand the different constraints based on the analysis of the access patterns, the workload, the application flow, and the screen wireframes. Using a diagramming tool like Hackolade Studio facilitates the conversation with non-technical stakeholders and helps reduce the time-to-market of application development efforts.

3. **Data tends to outlive applications by a wide margin:** it might be tempting to think that application code is where schemas are documented and quality is enforced. But data is probably shared by multiple applications, plus the livespan of applications is much shorter than for data. Hence it is critical to ensure a shared understanding of the meaning and context of data beyond a single application. Data modeling and schema design for MongoDB help achieve this objective.

Index